BILL DUKE

MY 40-YEAR

CAREER

ON SCREEN

AND BEHIND

THE CAMERA

BILL DUKE

ROWMAN & LITTLEFIELD
Lanham • Boulder • New York • London

Published by Rowman & Littlefield
An imprint of The Rowman & Littlefield Publishing Group, Inc.
4501 Forbes Boulevard, Suite 200, Lanham, Maryland 20706
www.rowman.com

Unit A, Whitacre Mews, 26-34 Stannary Street, London SE11 4AB

Distributed by NATIONAL BOOK NETWORK

British Library Cataloguing in Publication Information Available

Library of Congress Cataloging-in-Publication Data Available

ISBN 9781538105566 (electronic) | ISBN 9781538105559 (cloth : alk. paper)

♾™ The paper used in this publication meets the minimum requirements of American National Standard for Information Sciences—Permanence of Paper for Printed Library Materials, ANSI/NISO Z39.48-1992.

Printed in the United States of America

To my mother, Ethel Duke,
and my father, William H. Duke.

To not the wisdom seekers but those who,
in spite of losses, defeats, accomplishments, and victories,
constantly ask the question "Why?"

To all those who say "no"
when they were told to say "yes."

To all those who have the courage to live their dreams and
accept the consequences of those decisions.

To the impractical ones who play instruments, sing, or dance;
the ones who catch our hearts on global stages
and make us weep, wonder, laugh, and reflect on the whys of their lives.

To my grandfather and grandmother,
who gave up their dreams and encouraged us to live out our own.

To those who have the courage to stand up to challenges
that deal with race, gender, and ethnicity
and who do not allow those challenges and obstacles of this world
to stop them from doing what is right.

To those who are told, whether out of love or doubt,
"this cannot be done," "stop dreaming," or "that is impossible"
and still keep believing they can.

CONTENTS

PART IV: MY CAREER

PART V: NO CONCLUSIONS

ACKNOWLEDGMENTS

I WANT TO THANK MY FATHER and mother, Bill and Ethel Duke, who, through example, encouraged my sister and me to work and not to beg anybody for anything. I'd like to acknowledge my relatives who supported me through my self-doubt as a youth. I'd to thank to my sister Yvonne Hampton and my niece Nalo Hampton, two of my biggest supporters. I'd like to acknowledge Dutchess Community College, Roosevelt High School, and Mrs. Walker for encouraging me to continue to write. I'd like to thank Ms. Constance Kuhn, who gave me my first role in a play, *Emperor Jones*, when I was in Dutchess Community College. I'd like to thank Lloyd Richards and all the instructors at Boston University who gave me the insight, wisdom, and understanding into the craft of acting.

I'd like to thank my teachers and mentors at New York University: Michael Miller, Israel Hicks, and Michael Schultz, among many others. They pushed me to be better than I thought I could be. Lloyd Richards in particular was a mentor to me and gave me so much that I cannot begin to thank him enough. He was a great giver and sacrificer. Michael Schultz trusted me with my first real feature film break in *Car Wash* with Richard Pryor and many other stars. Of course, I have to acknowledge Joel Silver and Arnold Schwarzenegger for the roles I played in *Commando* and *Predator*. I want to thank all the folks at Disney for allowing me to direct *Cemetery Club* and *Sister Act II*, which gave me a major break in directing. I'd like to thank all the folks at MGM who supported me through *Hoodlum*. I'd like to thank David Jacobs, who gave me my first break in directing television, unknowingly, on *Knots Landing*. I want to thank Gilbert Moses, who gave me my first break as a Broadway actor. I want to thank my goddaughter, Nathalie, for being the most beautiful spirit who encouraged me and loved me unconditionally, and her mother, Anna. I want to thank all the wonderful women in my life, even though there are many I didn't treat with total regard. They loved me and cared for me.

I want to thank Chiijmree Williams, Dave Smitherman, and Diane Nine, who helped me put this entire adventure together. I'd like to thank my fans who still to this day recognize me and appreciate my accomplishments. I'd like to acknowledge myself for being able to keep God in my soul and in my spirit with meditation, prayer, and understanding. Last and most importantly, I'd like to thank God. I don't know what God looks like, but I know what God feels like, and I know that God has been there for me my entire life. I am still here because there are things left for me to do. Some people think thanking God is corny and overdone, and for those people I want to say *Thank God. Thank God. Thank God. Thank God.*

INTRODUCTION

I HAVE NEVER REALLY FIT IN. I probably never will because, in truth, I am a contradiction. I've always asked "Why?" I even wanted that to be the title of this book, because it's the title of my ongoing life journey and my evolving self, a process I believe never ends. Since birth and throughout my childhood, I innocently and repeatedly asked the question: "Why?" Mommy whys! Daddy whys! Teacher whys! Preacher whys! I think that we should always ask why. I was often reprimanded for asking questions. For me, "Why" is no longer a question, but a statement and affirmation of my existence.

My journey has not been easy. The difficulty of being born a black man in America at a time when segregation was firmly embedded in our lives always will remain a part of my reality. I was regularly and commonly called horrible, demeaning names. Those words caused deep, injurious wounds that took me to places of great darkness: places of hatred against others who showed hatred toward me; excuses that grew from mistrust of myself and others; violence that used the color of my skin and my ethnicity as an excuse for not accomplishing; violence of self-deprecation; anger toward women; self-injury that comes from the bottomless pit of low self-esteem; and the violence of justifying unjustifiable behaviors because I was born poor and black in America. To me, God was a vile, white-faced monster who had allowed me to be born into a life of chaos and unfair torture. I felt like I had a right to hate, resent, and self-destruct. I no longer believed in Him or myself. I hated God.

When I made it to Hollywood, I met and worked with stars like Andy Garcia, Laurence Fishburne, Oprah Winfrey, Whoopi Goldberg, Lauryn Hill, Tim Roth, Forest Whitaker, Olympia Dukakis, Kevin Hart, Arnold Schwarzenegger, Jesse Ventura, 50 Cent, Common, Mel Gibson, Snoop

Dogg, Dr. Dre, Whitney Houston, Ellen Burstyn, Larry Hagman, Vanessa Williams, Queen Latifah, and many others, including the casts and crews of TV shows including *Falcon Crest*, *Knots Landing*, *Hill Street Blues*, and *Dallas*.

Despite my successes, I endured the brutality of an industry that challenges the very nature of your existence and often rewards you with only critiques. I experienced career and financial ups and downs. I survived a battle with drugs that ultimately drove me to panhandling on the streets of New York and stealing food from the A&P supermarket.

Some of my friends went to work for IBM and other corporations. They had houses, mortgages, car notes, food, insurance, happy marriages, bitter divorces. Some worked at jobs they hated and some at jobs they loved. Many gave up their dreams to become responsible parents, husbands, wives, grandfathers, grandmothers, great-grandmothers, and great-grandfathers so that they could pass down legacies of tradition to the young.

I chose a different path: the path of the renegade, the rebel, the chance-taking, sometimes-starving, not-guaranteed, barely-making-it self-doubter, the irresponsible, the criticized, the foolish, the madman. I chose the impracticality of living a life filled with the passion of the creative. For this, I have paid the price.

Many undeserved crowns have been placed upon my head. Relationships have suffered because of my dedication to my work. Even today, I still wrestle with self-doubt, lack of fulfillment, and the questioning of the inquisitive. Fortunately, I am ultimately fulfilled by a life that I was not instructed to live, but one I choose to live.

PROLOGUE

IN DECEMBER 1982, WITH SEVERAL EPISODES of *Flamingo Road, Falcon Crest*, and other television shows under my belt, I made my way to CBS Studios to direct my first episode of the prime-time soap opera of that time, *Dallas*. Although *Falcon Crest* was a top-ten hit in its own right, *Dallas* was the holy grail of television. An opportunity to direct an episode of the number-one prime-time show—in its third year at the top of the ratings—was confirmation that I had proven my skills.

At 8:00 a.m., I drove to the studio lot for my first day of work. When I arrived at the gate, the large white security guard asked, "Who are you delivering for?"

"I'm sorry?" I replied.

"I said, 'Who are you *delivering for?*'"

I looked at the guard for what felt like an eternity. My mind flashed back to some of the many insults I had endured in my youth. I had been called *nigger, coon, blackie, darkie,* and *tar baby,* among other things, and in that moment it felt like little had changed.

When that guard asked me who I was delivering for, I wanted to respond, *I'm seriously considering delivering a can of whoop-ass to you, and I'm thinking about just how violently I want to deliver it.* But I sat in silence and stared at the guard's smug face as I remembered a speech that I had watched Dr. Martin Luther King Jr. deliver, during which he spoke passionately about the importance of a forgiving attitude.

After a few moments of reflection and great restraint, I calmly stated to the guard, "There is obviously a misunderstanding. I am the first black director on *Dallas,* the number-one hit show on television, and what I'm delivering is my expertise and talent to that show."

The slight gasp that escaped from the guard's lips was satisfying as he stared back at me. Finally, he opened the gate and let me pass.

Without Dr. King's sacrifices, I would have never been at that gate, and I would have never directed that episode of *Dallas*. Without Dr. King's words, that security guard may not have survived that moment. Without Dr. King, I don't think my career would have even been possible.

Part I

CHILDHOOD

Me in a baby carriage. *From the author's collection*

Chapter 1

WYATT JONES BEER GARDEN

The journey of a thousand miles begins with one step.—Lao Tzu

GOING OUT

Going out with nothing
Is the same as
Staying in.
You never meet
Anybody
And you don't know
Where you've been.
Going out with nothing
To give or understand
Is the same as
Talking to yourself
Or
Shaking your own hand.
People need to feel each other
Giving up themselves
To the
Day-to-day experience.
Break out of shells
And
Reach thru the silence
To

Soothe each other's pain
With
Wordless conversations
And
Risk loss and
Gain
Going out with nothing
Fools no one but
Yourself because
Everybody's listening
Waiting
For you
To share your wealth.
But
To hear a soul that's bankrupt
In words that are not felt
To remember nothing that's been said
Is like
Dead men talking to the dead
The only things worth saying
Are the things we
Feel
And whether they are wrong or right
Is not the question
Not tonight
When darkness covers everything
Even answers poets bring
But
Going out with nothing
Is the same as staying in
You never meet anybody
And
You don't know
Where
You've been!

I WAS BORN IN POUGHKEEPSIE, NEW YORK, on Friday, February 26, 1943, to Ethel Duke of West Point, Mississippi, and William H. Duke Sr. of Orange, Virginia. A few weeks after I was born, my mother's mother died. My baby eyes saw Mama drop to the floor screaming and Daddy consoling her. My mother's father, mother, and sister all died within a year of my birth.

A year later, my sister Yvonne was born. We lived in a two-bedroom apartment on the second floor above Wyatt Jones Beer Garden. We loved bath time. For our baths, Mama would take water from the top of the wood-burning stove, mix it with cold water, pour it into a big, round tin tub, and add soap. We were washed from head to toe, scrubbed, and scraped with black soap with water poured all over us.

Those times were filled with laughter as Mama tickled our little bodies before wrapping us in warm blankets and putting on homemade pajamas. On the weekends, our family would go downstairs to Wyatt Jones Beer Garden. We'd sit at the same corner table and see folks come in dressed to the nines. A jukebox played the music of Ella Fitzgerald, Louis Armstrong, Duke Ellington, Count Basie, and others. Folks did a dance called the swinging slop as they drank beer and straight whiskey shots. My sister and I would watch Mama and Daddy do the jigaboo dance and the slow grind and finally the slop. We would laugh as we sipped our Coca-Colas.

Sometimes, the owner, Mr. Jones, would call to us. "Sissy and Dukie, come on to the dance floor!" Yvonne and I would go to the middle of the floor and they'd put music on the juke. We would dance and twirl and spin and jump and laugh to the applause of the grown-ups that surrounded us. At the end of our dance, we would take our cup around to everybody and they would put in whatever they could afford.

My paternal grandfather was my savior. He sheltered me from the turmoil at home. He was my protection from their eyes of regret. Grandpa took me to places like the circus and the carnival, leading me by the hand past clowns, elephants, tigers, horses, and the sweet smells of cotton candy and popcorn mixed with the stench of animal dung stuck to the bottom of our shoes.

I was in a fantasy world far away from the pain of loss. It was now a world of wild animals trained to obey the whip of the master lion tamer. This world had rides in the sky and cars that bumped into each other amid the squeals of delighted children full of candy corn and sweet drinks. Grandpa's forehead kisses and protective embrace gave me permission to enjoy the controlled chaos without fear or dread. He was my protection from the troubles at home. He was my hero.

Mama and Daddy were forced to work long hours to make ends meet and support the family. That strong work ethic was admirable, but it also took its toll on the relationship. Sometimes they were kind to each other. Sometimes they would take out their frustrations on one another and I heard it all. My salvation came in the form of Grandpa's strength, his tenderness, his caring, and the safety I felt being held in his strong arms. Simply knowing that he would do anything to protect his grandbaby made me feel beyond special.

One day, Grandpa didn't come to my room like he usually did so I went to look for him. He wasn't downstairs. I called his name, but there was no answer. I asked Mama and Daddy where Grandpa was. Daddy said, "He's dead and he's not coming back." With so much loss around us, that's how my parents dealt with tragedy—directly and matter-of-factly.

I think it was their coping mechanism, a way to compartmentalize that which they could not control. Their focus was on our survival. I was not of the same mind. I couldn't believe my rock was gone. I cried for months; I cried until it felt like I had no more tears. Grandpa was gone, and I would have to continue without him. There was silence forevermore.

THE WORKERS

After the loss of Grandpa, I focused more on Mama and Daddy and I realized that they did an amazing job providing for us. They would never consider taking welfare or handouts of any kind—their pride just wouldn't allow it. They worked their way through the pain. That was their survival technique. Daddy was six-foot-one and very fit. He was a boxer who used to fight at a club in New York City. Daddy could stand straight up and, in one swift movement, kick the light bulb out of the socket on the ceiling.

My parents were not lecturers; instead, they taught by example. They worked hard and expected the same from their children. We cleaned the house, took out the garbage, and started cooking at a young age. We had to prepare complete meals like turkey with gravy, greens, turnips, mashed potatoes, and dessert. Working was a necessity, and if we complained that meant a whipping. Daddy worked at De Laval Separator Company. In peacetime, they made milk separator machines that removed the cream from cow's milk; in wartime, they made shells for gunships. Daddy worked in the foundry, and Mama, Yvonne, and I picked him up every day at 5:00 p.m.

If we were early, we would peer through the small window of the foundry and watch the men work. They wore metal masks with glass shields, thick coats, rubber aprons, gloves, and dusty boots as protection from the sparks of molten metal as it was poured into molds. The foundry was filled with thick, heavy smoke and scorching heat. The men's hands were marked with angry blisters and black-singed fingernails.

Despite the harsh conditions, I would often see them laughing and playfully punching each other. I watched them smile through their cigarette-stained teeth and heard the laughs that often turned to coughing fits as their lungs struggled to manage the daily abuse of alcohol and unfiltered Camels. I would get so excited when Daddy would glance over and point us out to the other guys. They would wave in our direction as Daddy clocked out.

Mama worked in the Hudson River State Hospital, which was a mental facility. We even knew some of the patients because they were neighbors or family members. Many issues stemmed from men coming back from the war with no acceptable outlet for their internal rage. Domestic violence was more common than anyone wanted to admit. Some beatings were from anger that stemmed from the loss of childhood dreams, and others the result of the horrors soldiers witnessed on Korean battlefields. There was also frustration after those war heroes returned home to restaurants and bars that denied them entry because of the color of their skin.

Some of those men never got recognition for their military sacrifice and service. That resentment turned into anger and distrust that was often taken out on those closest to them. For most, the only thing they had left was pride. Their pride was in the shoes they wore, their suits, their expensive hats, the number of children they had, and the cars they drove.

If they did end up at the local hospital, Mama listened to their concerns and comforted them as best she could. When she came home, she'd tell us stories of people hanging themselves and others who sat motionless, retreating into their own damaged minds. Mama was a practical nurse with no formal nursing training and no degree. Mama had a degree in caring. As she washed their sheets and changed their diapers, she would listen to their stories and make them feel valued and important once again.

If Mama and Daddy didn't have to work on the weekends, we were sometimes told to go put on our pajamas. Yvonne and I knew that meant we were going to the movies and then straight to bed once we got home. At the theater, the first thing we saw were live musicians that often played as the seats filled. Then we would watch the newsreels and finally the movie. I was able to shut everything else out and disappear into those stories as they unfolded on the silver screen. After the movies, we would climb in the bed with Mama and Daddy and they would read the funny papers to us to make us laugh.

Holidays in our home were either heavily celebrated or treated like an ordinary day. There was no between. When Christmas rolled around, Daddy would always wait until the last minute to buy a tree. Daddy wasn't cheap, but he was frugal. He loved making money more than spending it. Christmas was no big deal for us, because we knew we would get only underwear and socks.

My dad always made it clear that his family came first. Everyone ended up at our house when they needed help. Our door was always open. Though my parents were kind to everyone else, many times they were not kind to each other. Daddy didn't raise his voice when he was angry with Mama. He would whisper things to her, and she would throw things. They fought bitterly, and then they cried. Their love was scarred by words that cut deep into the flesh of trust yet endured long after the sound of slamming doors had faded. They cursed, smashed light bulbs, and eventually there were bloody teeth and noses to accompany the screams of rage and pain. That hostility spilled over into our birthdays, Christmases, and unholy days. It spilled into our dollhouses, Howdy Doody dolls, and toy trucks. We did not have the luxury of innocence.

We got our beatings from Daddy, but when Mama was mad she would pick up something and throw it at us. Daddy would talk first, and then he'd tell us to find a switch from a tree outside. I would think *maybe I'll break a leg before I get back there*. I would try to trick him by finding the weakest branch, so he could hit me only once or twice before it snapped. Then Daddy started watching out of the window, which meant that strategy no longer worked.

FIRST LOVE

In 1948, I was five years old and had fallen in love with my next-door neighbor. Her name was Nancy. She was blonde with blue eyes and a kind smile. I would sit in the dirt with my best friend, Pepper Boome, and we would make mud cakes with Nancy, Nancy's sister, and my sister Yvonne. We'd bring water down from the apartment or gather it from rain puddles and argue over who had the best-tasting mud cake. Yvonne would try to put them in my mouth and I would do the same to her. Sometimes we would shape the mud into people or animals. We smeared each other's faces so by the end of it, we looked like little human mud cakes.

There was an old white woman who lived on the other side of us and she was wicked. She was probably in her eighties and she did not like black people—or children for that matter—so she especially hated black children. She'd call us "little coonies" and tell us to get away from her yard. We'd put mud on our faces and then sing and dance in front of her just to bother her. We knew that getting on her nerves was an easy thing to do, whether it was standing too close to her fence, dripping mud into her yard, or singing loudly so she could tell us "niggies" to shut up. It felt strange to discover that she hated us just because of our color. Nancy and her sister were confused because she hated them, as well, and they were white, but they played with us, so in the lady's mind they were niggies too. Racism and hatred are rarely logical.

One summer day, I was in the backyard drawing pictures of Nancy when she came out of her back door and asked me what I was doing.

I said, "I'm drawing a picture."

She asked me, "A picture of who?"

"A picture of you," I said. She looked at the picture.

"My hair doesn't look like that." She gave the picture back and gently touched my face with her soft hand.

Just then, her mother called her to get in the car and go to the store. Just like that, she was gone. I had never felt the touch of a hand on my face except from Mama and Daddy. Sometimes Aunt Beulah would kiss my cheek and pinch my face, but the touch of Nancy's hand was different. It was electric.

For my first day of kindergarten, Mama and Daddy bought me new shoes, pants, a shirt, and a striped tie. They told me I was handsome and that I would get a whippin' if they heard that I smart-mouthed the teacher. We walked to the bus stop along with Nancy and her mother. It was her first day, too. I got on the bus with Nancy, but she did not sit with me. I turned around and saw that she was talking to boys, white boys, who were bigger than me. Those boys looked at me with angry eyes, and I turned back around in my seat. This Nancy was a stranger to me, the only little colored boy on the bus.

When we arrived at Violet Avenue Elementary, the assistant teacher ushered us off the bus and to our classroom. I set my book bag down at my desk. The teacher asked each of us to stand, introduce ourselves, and shake each other's hand. As the children passed by, I got no handshakes. Nancy shook everyone's hand but mine. I felt lonely and confused. When I looked over at Nancy, the same boy from the bus was sitting next to her. The teacher asked each of us to stand up and say our names. When I stood, I was nervous.

She repeated her request, "Young man, what is your name?"

"Duke," I said.

"Is that your first name or your last name, young man?"

"Bill Duke," I said. The other children laughed.

At lunchtime, I sat alone at a table on the school playground. A group of white children, including Nancy, surrounded me and mocked the classroom incident.

One boy said to another, "What is your name, young man?"

The other boy said, "Duke."

The first boy said, "Is that your first name or your last name?"

"Bill Duke."

"I'm confused. I thought your name was nigger."

"No, ma'am, that's not true. My name is black nigger." All the children laughed. Nancy laughed, too. I never spoke to Nancy again.

After school I got off the bus and ran home crying. I shoved past my parents and hurried into the bathroom. I took my clothes off, sat in the bathtub, turned on the water, and put Bab-O cleanser on a sponge to scrub the black off my body. I tried hard to scrub away the pain, the hurt, and the rejection. I realized nothing was happening, so I decided to try mother's bleach. After all, she used it to make the white towels whiter, so it should work on me. Just as I was about to drink the bleach, my parents burst into the bathroom to check on me. I told them what I was trying to do and why I was doing it. My mother and my sister cried with me, but my father's face turned to stone with anger.

GRANDMA AND FISHING

Some weekends when Mama and Daddy wanted a break, they would take us down to Catherine Street to Grandma Sadey Duke's house. I dreaded going to that house because it was strangely dark most of the time, and there was always a new, unidentifiable odor. Grandma was a kindhearted, compassionate woman who loved us, but the scary part was that when she smiled, we saw gums but no teeth.

One day we asked her where her teeth were, and she said, "In the jar next to my bed. Dukie, why don't you go get them for your grandmother?" I looked at Yvonne for help but found none. So slowly I approached the narrow stairway that led up to Grandma's room. The wooden banister was partially cracked. Some steps had carpeting, and others did not. There was no light in the stairwell. It was a slow journey, but finally I reached the top. I entered the bedroom filled with clothes, papers, boxes, various colored wigs, scarves, fans, and a coal stove tucked in the corner. To my left, in a glass jar atop a small table next to the bed, were indeed Grandma's teeth. There was no lid on the jar, and the liquid inside looked thick and gooey. I was seven years old, and in my mind, the teeth were looking at me. So I extended my arm, picked up the jar, and hurried down the stairs.

Grandma said, "Thank you, baby. Now set them down here on the table next to me." Then she reached into the jar and grabbed the bottom teeth. She slipped them into her mouth and the slimy liquid dribbled down her chin. I looked at Yvonne, and she started to cry. Grandma asked, "What's wrong, baby?" Then she did the same with the top teeth and smiled at us. "So how do I look now?" Yvonne cried even harder.

"You look nice, Grandma," I replied.

"Now, both of y'all come over here and give Grandma a kiss." Yvonne had a look of terror as I pushed her toward Grandma. After she was finished with Yvonne, she grabbed me in her arms so quickly that I couldn't escape her. I closed my eyes and felt her moist mouth on my skin. Then she took us to the kitchen and asked if we were hungry. We both immediately said no.

"Now, you childrens know better than that. You know you have to eat and stay healthy so you don't catch that polio." She opened the oven door, removed the wig that had been drying, and plopped it right on her head. Then she prepared our lunch using the same oven. We had to eat every bit of food put on our plates because "poor folks don't waste no food."

Dad's father was a tobacco farmer who owned property and even had a maid. When Grandfather died, they sold the property and moved to Poughkeepsie. After many years of working very hard and living over Wyatt Jones, my father bought us a house that was a total fixer-upper. There was no front porch, no paint on the walls, and the yard was a half-acre of dirt. My father didn't see what it was, but what it could be. He enlisted the help of Uncle Howard, Uncle Albert, and Uncle Jimmie, and the four of them used their bare hands to turn that shack into a home. They even renovated two barns and then filled them with pigs that would be slaughtered in the fall.

To pay for the new house, Dad spent more than twice as many hours at the De Laval Separator Company and Mom worked overtime in the hospital. Daddy also butchered and cured his own meat. For the winter, Mama would can foods from the garden and store meat and fish in the freezer. At twelve and thirteen years old, Yvonne and I had to raise the pigs that were kept in the barn behind the house. We would wash and feed them, remove the feces-packed hay, and keep the place as clean as possible. We liked the pigs and the pigs liked us, so we gave them names. The white pigs were called "Whitey," the black pigs were called "Blackey," and the spotted pigs were called "Spotty." We used to talk to them as we did our chores and then chase them afterward. They would squeal and so would we.

We used to get angry when it came time to kill our friends. We'd cry from our bedroom windows as we watched Daddy and my uncles string the pigs up from the tree. We saw the pigs shot in the head and then split open. Once the pigs were butchered, they were put into barrels of salt, pepper, and molasses. After the liquid drained, the meat was hung to dry and cure in the cellar. Mold would cover the pig parts after a couple weeks.

Sometimes my sister and I would go to the cellar to try to figure out which parts were Spotty, Whitey, and Blackey. We'd talk about how mean Dad had been to sacrifice our friends. Later on in the winter while enjoying our bacon and ham breakfast, Dad would say, "You know that bacon you're eating? You're eating Spotty right now!"

Every few weeks, on a Saturday, my father and uncles used to rent a boat to go fishing. We would go to different lakes around Poughkeepsie, and I was asked to join them when I was around eight years old. I didn't know why I was there because I didn't understand fishing. I didn't understand why they were so happy about catching fish. I didn't like anything about it. Putting the worm on the hook was horrible. I thought I could hear the worm scream. When the fish was pulled into the boat, it would wiggle and flop around until they smashed its head. I cried because I didn't understand. "Why are you killing the worms and the fish?" I asked. Uncle Albert laughed, "So you can eat, boy." I'd suggest we just have pancakes. "You ain't got to kill pancakes. You ain't got to kill rice. If there were pancakes, eggs, toast, jam, peanut butter, fruits, and vegetables, why did we have to kill fish and chickens and pigs and cows? They were alive." Their explanation was, "someday you'll understand." Later, I became vegetarian for many years.

FIRST HOUSE RULES

We loved our new house at 56 Fallkill Avenue because we had our own rooms and more space to play. Four times a year the circus would march down our street and Daddy would put my sister or I on his shoulders so we could watch the horses, elephants, and other animals pass while lively music played in the background. Not many things could top a circus when we were young, and it reminded me of the fun times with Grandpa before he passed away.

Yvonne and I were always getting in some sort of trouble. One day, after we finished hitting and chasing each other, we decided to create an adventure. We got a five-gallon gas can out of the garage and poured it into the garbage hole that was dug in the ground. We threw lit matches in the hole, but nothing happened at first. Then we got a rag and wrapped it around a stick, lit it, and threw it in. We ran into the house and turned around when we heard a huge explosion. Our neighbors came running to see if we were okay. We acted as if we never heard anything.

Mrs. Johnson, our next-door neighbor, had twenty-one children at her house, and she would sit on the stoop for most of the day and watch the neighborhood. My father and mother told Mrs. Johnson that Yvonne and I were not to ride our bikes in the street, but only on the sidewalk. One day, Mrs. Johnson saw us riding our bikes in the street. She screamed at the top of her lungs, "Yvonne! Dukie! Come here right now!" She took us by our collars and plopped us down on the brown couch in her living room while her spotted dog stared at us. As Mrs. Johnson dialed Daddy at work, Yvonne and I begged her, "Please don't call Daddy. We won't do it again, Mrs. Johnson. We will clean your yard. We won't do it again. Please!"

All the while, the dog sat there watching us with eyes of compassion. After speaking with Daddy, Mrs. Johnson hung up the phone. Then she looked at us and asked, "Y'all want something to drink?"

We said, "No, ma'am."

"How about some cake?"

"No, ma'am."

"Cornbread?"

"No, ma'am."

"Well, I guess we just gon' sit here then."

Mrs. Johnson hummed to Mahalia Jackson songs while we sat and watched the clock of doom. There was a knock at the door.

"Hello, Mrs. Johnson. How are you today?"

"Fine, Mr. Duke. Well, here they are."

"Thank you, Mrs. Johnson. Come on, y'all. Let's go."

Daddy walked down the street silently, with us behind him, up the driveway into the barn where we put our bikes. My father in his work clothes, hands blistered and rough, took us into the house and made us sit on the couch.

"Now, you know why you gettin' this whippin', right?"

"We didn't mean it, Daddy," I said.

"You know I asked you not to ride your bikes in the street because cars come speeding all the time and y'all could get hit. You know I told you, right?"

"But Dukie made me do it!"

"No, Yvonne made me do it! We're sorry, Daddy."

"You sorry about what?"

"We sorry we rode our bikes on the street."

"Yes, Daddy and we will never do it again."

"Alright, you promise?"

"Yes, we promise. We will never ride in the street again."

"I believe you. Okay, now go outside and pick a switch and bring it back inside for your whippins."

Chapter 2

LITTLE BLACK SAMBO

You can run, you can hide; but you can never escape what's inside.
—Bill Duke

OUR HEARTS WERE GREEN

The pie of life
Is served
In slices
Too hot
For some lips
And
Once burned
Forever turned away
From
Treats of unknown qualities
For once fear
Rises in the heart
There is no end
Of
Wondering
No end
Of
Avoiding hands
And eyes
And thoughts

And listening
For
We
Will not
Try again
Again
We will not
Try
Again
So
The flag
Is all
We've known
And
All
We've ever seen
We
Fear our dreams
Of
Waking
For
Our hearts
Are green

———————

MY THIRD-GRADE TEACHER MADE SURE WE knew that history was an important part of our learning. During history week, she taught us that without a past, there would be no present. She held up pictures of George Washington, Thomas Jefferson, Benjamin Franklin, Abraham Lincoln, and others. It was a visual celebration of the contribution of the great leaders to whom she thought we should pay homage.

Then, looking at me and the other boy of color, she said, "Please don't think that I have left you out, because there is greatness in your past also." First, she held up a picture of George Washington Carver and told us about his peanut contribution and its significance. The only other picture she showed was the cover of an illustrated book entitled *Little Black Sambo*.

In the book, Little Black Sambo ran around the tree being chased by tigers. His eyes were impossibly wide. He was bug-eyed. His teeth were frozen in a terrified smile. Fear stood his hair straight up on the top of his head. He ran so hard and so fast that the tigers chasing him eventually turned to butter. After showing it to us, my teacher gave us a smile of satisfaction, a smile of recognition, a guiltless smile of the unaware. When I got home, I told my father what happened and asked, "Why didn't you tell me that's how they made butter?" When my parents heard that my teacher celebrated *Little Black Sambo* as a part of Negro history, they were very upset.

As I look back now, I realize that it was not the teacher's conscious attempt to diminish my significance or the significance of any other people of color in the class. She truly believed there was no difference between George Washington Carver and Little Black Sambo. These were the only significant black contributors she knew. It was simply her honest effort based on the fundamental ignorance that formed the very fabric of our world in upstate New York at that time.

It was the ignorance of assumption—not of intentional malice—but an expectation of privilege and assumed superiority. We were recognized but our true worth was unrecognizable, and a lack of recognition leaves subconscious scars that you carry in your lunchbox every day. When you open your lunchbox and unwrap the sandwich that your mother so carefully packed, your peanut butter and jelly or your Spam never tasted quite as good.

Life in Poughkeepsie meant rain-soaked autumns and hot summers filled with mosquitos, bugs, and ants. Church was an important part of life. There were church services of praise, shouts, and oversized women wearing oversized hats passing out from enthusiasm and eased back to consciousness with huge, multicolored fans and cups of cold water.

Screams of *Jesus!* and *Hallelujah!* punctured the air as the choir sang emotional confirmation that Jesus was our Lord and Savior, that God would take away all pain and sorrow, that without Jesus there was no living. Taking communion meant sipping cups of grape juice that represented the blood of our Lord and Savior and eating the small crackers that represented the body of Christ.

Our Baptist church housed so much more than worship: preachers as gods, deacons on boards, usher boards, boards of trustees, women's club, men's clubs, youth clubs, dartball clubs, souls being saved, and confessions being vomited. There was endless begging for the grace of forgiveness: begging for another chance, begging for salvation and the strength to make it through another day, begging for all that makes the soul come to a place of peace, begging to not be worried by the challenges of marriage betrayal and forms of adultery, begging to recover the indulgence of last night's drunken stupor. Begging was followed by *forgive us Father, for we know not what we do.* Forgiveness. Forgiveness. Forgiveness.

Mrs. Williams sat in the choir. She was in her sixties and close to three hundred pounds. Yvonne and I nicknamed her "Hoggy Hanna." When my parents could not attend church because they were hungover from their Saturday-night stupor of liquor, song, dance, and sex heard through the thin walls, our next-door neighbor Mrs. Williams would take us to church. She would drive us and sing along the way to practice for her morning solo. Her voice was like a screech of repentance. My sister and I sat close in the backseat pinching each other on the legs to keep from laughing at Hoggy Hanna's singing voice.

First, we were taken to Sunday school, where we learned Bible lessons, and then we were ushered upstairs for the church service. We sat in the rows just behind the missionary women dressed all in white with big hats that obstructed our view. My parents instructed Hoggy Hanna to report any misbehaving. If she heard us whispering, she would stare down the pews with a scowl. We laughed at her screeching choir solo and tried to hold back the bubbly laughter, ducking our heads behind the pew so that Hoggy Hanna would not see us. After church, we sat in the backseat in silence, terrified of what was to come. She'd look in the rearview mirror. We could see her eyes peering at us without blinking.

When arrived home, if we had behaved she would smile, kiss us on our foreheads, and tell our parents, "You have some good and well-behaved childrens." If we had given her trouble, she would say, "The devil's spirit gots 'em today!"

As she closed the door behind her, we were spanked into cries and promises that we would never do it again. We hated Hoggy Hanna. We never wished her any ill will or harm, but when she was unable to make it to church and her seat was empty, we felt a sense of relief and hopefulness that her illness would last several Sundays.

We would go grocery shopping at the A&P supermarket. Although she could cook well, Mama had two jobs, so sometimes dinner wasn't ready. Occasionally, we'd stop at Howard Johnson's restaurant to pick up burgers, fries, hot dogs, fried chicken, rice, green beans, lemon meringue pie, and as Daddy called them, "smashed potatoes" with milkshakes, Coca-Cola, ginger ale, and Pepsi. Whether she cooked it or not, to Mama the most important thing was that we all had dinner at the table and that we thanked God for the food and family.

We preferred it when Daddy prayed 'cause Daddy's prayers were short and sweet. *Thank God for this food and this day. Amen.* But Mama would go on. *Thank God for letting us wake up every morning, clothed in our right mind. Thank God for our childrens, Sissy and Dukie. Thank God for Mommy and Daddy. Although they are gone, they're looking down on us right now protecting us from the darkness of this world. Thank Him for this food, bless the hands of the cook, and bless those who have no food on this God-given day. Bless all the starving chilrens in Korea.*

THE DOGHOUSE BABYSITTER

We felt safe until the day when nothing would never be the same. She came to visit us without warning or regret. She was a young smile marked by gaps, a young smile that was always betrayed by the sad and painful eyes in her lined face. She was our babysitter. When she laughed, it was a laugh of tearful guilt. She was our protector, our guardian hired by hardworking parents. Her presence gave my parents the peace of mind to work late and earn for the family.

My father and uncles had built a doghouse in the backyard on the hill overlooking the half acre of green lawn. The doghouse was painted green with a gray-tiled roof. Yvonne liked it so much that she filled it with white-faced dolls, stuffed animals, and other toys. The dog didn't like that we had taken over his house, but it became our own personal sanctuary.

That doghouse was big enough for all of us—the babysitter, Yvonne, and me. It was where our babysitter would take us to play. She would read us books, make us laugh, and let us sleep. It was a magical place, but one day that spell was forever broken. As we slept, I felt a slight pressure and realized she was touching me in a place that had never been touched except by my mother's bathtub hands. This touch was not like that. I saw that my sister was also being violated. These were not the hands of love. They were hands of lust that touched and penetrated my sister's private parts as they cuddled mine.

That day, the doghouse held our horrible secret inside: kissing tongues and mouths, licking our faces with grunts and groans, touching us and forcing us to touch each other, threatening us to never tell our parents or anyone else, threatening us with death, pain, and regret while she smiled with eyes of anger.

That evening when my parents came home, our babysitter walked us hand in hand across the grass. My sister and I were crying so hard we could barely see. When we got to the bottom of the hill, my mother asked us what was wrong. We looked at the babysitter. I said to my mother, "Nothing, Mama. We're just hungry, right, Yvonne?" And my sister nodded her head yes.

Nothing was ever the same after that. Not that the grown-ups became our enemies, but my sister and I felt we could no longer trust the grown-ups. They became the gravediggers that would bury us in secrets, the kind of secrets we had not known before that day. We believed that if we told, the grown-ups would not believe us because we were not able to speak a language that they would accept as truth.

Yvonne and I saw each other differently, too. We didn't totally understand what had happened, but we thought we had done something wrong and somehow blamed each other for it. Every time the babysitter came to the house, a layer of shame would be added to our view of the world. I felt like I couldn't trust any adult, but especially women. They seemed mysterious and secretive and difficult for me to understand.

Fate intervened, and the babysitter arrived late one too many times, so my father decided to fire her and hire Wilbert, a young man who lived down at the end of Fallkill Avenue. With that one decision, Daddy unknowingly protected us from more episodes of unspeakable evil. I felt great relief but still found ladies very confusing. We had been taught that women were the caregivers who loved children and provided safety and comfort, so I didn't understand why that woman had subjected us to such horrible treatment. How dare she take from us the security our parents had worked so hard to instill! The old babysitter moved away. I wasn't sure where she went, but I hoped it was West Hell.

MEN LIKE ME (PART 1)

Men like me
Were raped as baby boys
By women babysitters our parents trusted with their trust
And our toys
They gently unzipped our pants
With puke words filled with perfume snot
Lust and ants
Made us feel there was something wrong with us
With our feelings our confusion our feelings our fears our disgust
Men like me

Chapter 3

UNDERSTANDING HATE

Hate and mistrust are the children of blindness.—William Watson

HOWEVER FLAWED THE CHURCH AND COMMUNITY center were, they were places that housed the old and young and their hopes for the future. My sister and I spent a great deal of time within the walls of Ebenezer Baptist Church. Those walls gave us the assurance that no matter what was happening in the world outside of Poughkeepsie, we were protected from the storms of racism and the evil of the unknown.

We would walk together to and from church, which was not far from our home. We were part of the dartball club, junior choir, the boys' club, the girls' club, and the junior this, that, and the other. It was all designed to keep us occupied and out of the troubled streets of Poughkeepsie, New York, in the 1950s. I was eleven years old and Yvonne was ten.

One Saturday after attending a youth church event, Yvonne and I passed three men in their twenties on motorcycles at a filling station on our walk home. They were leathered down, bare-armed biker men. One of them yelled out, "Where you goin', little niggers? We want to talk to you."

Mama and Daddy taught us to run from trouble as fast and hard as we could, especially if trouble was bigger than us. So I said to Yvonne, "Let's go!" We started walking fast. They yelled, "I said, niggas, where you goin'?" They crossed the street and ran after us. I felt a strong hand on my shoulder. "Yvonne, run faster!" She didn't listen. She stopped and watched as they knocked me to the ground, kicked me, stomped me, punched me, and spat on me. Yvonne cried "Stop! Stop!" I could say nothing. I was buried in the pain of boots, blood, and tears. Finally, one of the bikers held my head up and said, "You see, nigga, next time we wanna talk to you, you better stop. Do you understand?" When I did not respond, he grabbed my face harder and said, "Do you understand?" and I nodded.

As they were leaving, he wiped his hands on his pants. My sweat and blood smeared the denim. I got to my feet, grabbed my sister, and we ran all the way home. Once we got on the porch, we wept as we watched the beginnings of the coming storm. Inside, Yvonne grabbed Mama's apron and fell to her knees. I made my way to the couch in a zombie-like state to lie down. Mama asked what happened as she cleaned my face with a white rag and ice. I told her everything.

When my father got home and my mother told him, he ran upstairs and got his gun. He put me and my sister in the car while my mother screamed, "Don't do it. Don't do it. Bill, it won't make a difference." He drove down Smith Street to the corner garage where we had seen the bikers. Daddy got out of the car and went to the owner of the gas station. "Where are they?" The owner said they went up Main Street hours ago. Daddy got back in the car and slowly drove down Main Street. He looked in every store, parking lot, bar, and on every corner, searching for hours to no avail. He took the same drive every day for a week, pointing out men and asking us if they were the ones. Even if we had seen them, we were not going to tell my father because we knew that Mother's widow tears would haunt us forever.

Daddy was not a violent man, but he was a measured man who tolerated no disrespect toward himself or his family. Two years prior, two white policemen had pulled over my Daddy after he made an illegal U-turn. While ticketing him, one officer said, "You black coons should learn how to obey the white man's law." They laughed. My father replied, "Don't you see my family in this car?" And the officer responded, "All I see is monkeys."

My father opened the door and in one swift motion grabbed the officer's gun, threw it to the ground, punched him, knocked out the other officer, and stomped them both unconscious. The boxer inside of him came out that day, but he was not one to run from a problem. He got back in the car and drove us to the police station. My mother went inside with him and apparently my father explained to the chief of police what had occurred and said that even though he was wrong in making the U-turn, he allowed no one to disrespect him, his wife, or his children. Daddy was not arrested that day. In fact, the chief of police apologized and said he would not prosecute because the police officers would've done the same if someone had disrespected their families. From that day on, even though I was a young boy, I understood what manhood was.

Growing up, I was never popular. I was bigger and taller than most of the other kids. I was kind of nerdy and wasn't a great relationship person. I could get along from time to time, but girls didn't seem to like me that much. Hitting on girls was not only an embarrassment but a humiliation because they used to laugh in my face. I would say "how is your day going," "nice dress," "pretty stockings," "you smell good," and "my name is Bill." That was the extent of my eloquence. The confident boys obviously gave them a much more powerful dialogue, but for me, not so much. My first consensual sexual experience was when I was ten years old with Lois under the dining room table in my house. I didn't know what sex was, but Lois had kissed me on the bus and held my hand, leading me into my house after school. Nobody was home. We went under the dining room table. She put her tongue in my mouth and then pulled my pants down and put her mouth on my penis. I always wondered how she knew what to do and how to do it, because she was also ten. Until then, I had been touched only by my babysitter, so this was the first time I had been touched by a girl, by someone I wanted to touch me. I had an epiphany when she sucked on my penis. Stars exploded. My eyes closed and opened. My toes curled. I screamed silently as she bit me just a little bit. She took her panties off, put my penis in her vagina, and sat on it. Just before I was going to lurch, she jumped off and watched me squirt. She laughed and kissed me. "This is your first time, huh?" Before I could answer, Yvonne came in the house. "Mom. Dad. You here?" she said as she entered the kitchen and started making some food. Lois put her panties on and snuck quietly out the front door. When the door closed, my sister came from the kitchen and said, "Who's that? Where you been?" I looked at her. "What do you mean?"

I thought of sex as a game of pleasure from that day on, and maybe the reason I've hurt so many women in my life was because I always focused on the act, not the person. I liked having sex with different women, but I never went beyond that and made emotional connections. I simply enjoyed the physical act. Maybe it's because of the way I learned about sex; I'm not sure. First, it was a horrible experience, and then I found out it could be pleasurable. My main regret as an adult was that I never explained myself to the women who loved me. If they understood what I'd been through, maybe they wouldn't have hated me when I couldn't connect emotionally. It's interesting, as you get older, you see yourself differently and with a clearer understanding of your own humanity. Along the way, you figure out that you don't really understand as much as you thought.

I assumed that once I was older I would be able to pass along some of the things I had learned as I navigated through the world, but I don't know if I can because I continue to question everything. Why this and why that? Why do we keep doing the same things over and over again, expecting a different result? Why, if I'm so goddamn smart, do I continue to make stupid mistakes that I know are going to be harmful to me and the people I love? Why?

I am struggling to answer that because I love myself enough to want to improve, not just for me, but for the people who I love and who love me in return. In the meantime, I just remember Lois. She made me feel something that I never felt before or since.

MELLO

The moon melted softly on the trees
Breezes blew
The scent of lilacs thru the willow's hair
Fingers moved
Lips whispered
Ooooooooooooooo please please touch me there
Not in the morning
When
Snails and crickets hide beneath the leaves
But
In the moon
When darkness braids her hair
And
Spiders weave

Part II

A GROWING MIND

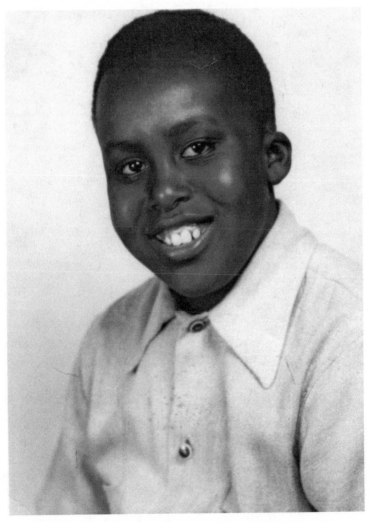

Me around twelve years old. *From the author's collection*

Chapter 4

FINDING THE SKIPS

Short as life is, we make it still shorter by the careless waste of time.
—Victor Hugo

IN MY EARLY TEENAGE YEARS, I was given the job of mowing our half-acre lawn for my weekly allowance. It was a massive lawn and mowing it by hand took around two hours every Saturday. When I finished mowing the lawn, I'd walk to the front porch where my father sat reading the morning paper and smoking his pipe. I'd tell him I was done. He would ask, "Are you sure?"

"Yes, sir, I'm sure."

"Let's go see."

Daddy would walk down the steps with heavy, weighted boots and head to the very back of the lawn. He'd walk every inch of the yard in search of what he called "skips"—patches of grass I had missed. I followed him, hoping he wouldn't find any skips. He always found some. He simply pointed at them, looked back at me and said, "You see?" I would have to go back and mow the entire lawn again. Once I was sure there weren't any more skips, my father walked the lawn again, then returned to the front porch, sat in his chair, looked me in my eyes, and said, "Now that's better," before reaching into his pocket to pull out my allowance. Then I was free.

At that time, I hated my father, or at least I thought I did. Sure, I made some mistakes. I wasn't perfect. I remember one time I asked my father what the big deal was about leaving skips in the lawn when all the neighbors had them, too. "Mr. Johnson next door has skips in his lawn. Mr. Anderson across the street has skips in his lawn, and so does Mrs. Meyers down the block, and nobody ever points theirs out. So why do I have to get all the skips all the time? I'm only human." My father then looked at me in steely silence.

After a long beat, he replied, "If you want to live in my house, you will not have skips in this lawn. If you want to have skips, you should go and live with the neighbors. You absolutely will not have any skips in my lawn. Do you understand that? Yes or no?"

"I understand," I replied. And that was that. Though I hated the control he had over me, it felt good when he couldn't find any skips. I didn't want to admit it, but it felt good to earn his approval because he had such high standards.

I had always liked things to be a certain way, and some people saw that as strange. They didn't understand that having no wrinkles in my pants or straightening pencils on my desk in perfect alignment was my way of controlling things, of restoring order to my chaotic teenage world. One day, I realized that chasing the perfect lawn had made quite an impact on me. The perennial pursuit of perfection was the lesson my father worked so hard to teach me. I grew to love him for keeping me focused and for not allowing me to do anything halfway. That skill was a key factor in my later successes.

CIVIL RIGHTS

The civil rights movement had begun, and like the rest of the country, our community struggled with the realities of desegregation. My sister and I were learning to navigate this new landscape of changing attitudes and those that refused to change. I had to find my identity as a young black man while watching my sister go through her challenges. There were many times we faced situations we did not know how to handle. My parents had seen the horrors of racial persecution for most of their lives, so they encouraged us to discuss the evolving attitudes toward our people. They helped us realize that we had an identity and that it had nothing to do with what other people thought about us. We were as valued and important as anyone else, regardless of skin color. Over time we learned how to stand up for ourselves. We were in a turbulent world and no one was coming to our rescue. My father and mother gave advice, but it was up to us to figure out how to handle each situation. They were clear that they never wanted us to get involved in violent situations unless there were no other options.

Because I was tall and dark, I was initially perceived as a threatening person. It was an odd feeling to watch someone I passed on the sidewalk move by quickly or even cross the street to avoid me. Initially, I tried to smile and appear friendly before they made their judgement, but no matter how much I tried to appear unassuming, it was no use. I was seen as a young, angry black man.

I became aggressive at times. Daddy had always taught us to stand up for ourselves, especially me, as a man of color. For a while, I was quick to fight anyone who tried to demean or take advantage of me, but I realized there needed to be a balance. I didn't want to feed into those stereotypes, so I had to learn to make peace with their ignorance. I would try to educate them through my words and actions. As long as they were respectful, I knew my father would be proud. It was important for us to remember our worth in a world where we were rarely treated equally.

My sister and I faced many challenges because of our dark complexions. Things would have been much different had we been light skinned, and it was a horrible reality to have our worth determined by skin tone. A darker complexion meant more bullying and less respect from whites *and* blacks. Light-skinned blacks were seen as being closer to the skin tone of the majority—the whites—and that was the ideal. That racial bias found its way into the black community, creating a similar dynamic. The lighter the skin, the better the treatment. It was difficult to not only deal with poor treatment from other races but from my own as well. My sister and I called the light-skinned blacks *uppity* and *snooty* until one day we met a family that changed our perception.

The Penfields were a group of kids who had been abandoned by their mother and father and put into an adoption shelter. My Uncle Charlie and Aunt Etta provided them with a stable home and we grew close to them. Although our skin tones were different, we had a lot in common with the Penfields. Because of the abuse they received from their mother and father, they trusted no one, not even my Uncle Charlie. He tried to get them to vent to him about the things they had endured but they refused. Yvonne and I bonded with them, though, and eventually we became friends. We cared for each other. We went to see them, and they came see us. We had the greatest times laughing, playing, and getting to know one another, which helped us see that the color differences of our skin didn't matter. We learned what life was like for them as they did for us, and we came to realize that all that mattered was how we treated each other.

I just wished everyone else understood that.

Uncle Charlie had a small garden and a chicken pen, and we went outside and fed the chickens when we visited. Aunt Etta would come out of the house, pick up a chicken by the neck, and swing it around until it went limp. Then she would put it on a wood block in the backyard, chop off its head, put the body in warm water, pick off the feathers, cut it open, take out the liver and intestine, and chop it into small pieces. Then we would eat it for lunch, just like the pigs my daddy used to kill.

DUKIE DUKE'S ROOM

My mother and father were admired among our relatives and were often called upon to provide advice, support, and occasionally a place to stay for an uncle or cousin who was down on his luck. That impacted me directly, because they often offered up "Dukie Duke's room." My room was nice, with two beds and a window. Because of the frequent guests, my belongings were usually pushed to a small corner beside my bed.

When Uncle Albert, my mom's brother, got a divorce and fell on hard times, he stayed in my room through much of my teen years. I loved Uncle Albert and the fact that he had been in World War II and fought for our nation. Unfortunately, he faced unimaginable discrimination when he returned home. He would tell me stories of battle, courage, and fear, and I loved imagining him as a brave soldier. Then there were other nights when I could hear him softly crying. He missed Aunt Carrie and he often talked about feeling like a failure. After he wiped away the tears, he would sit up in bed and smoke for hours, looking out the window at nothing in particular.

Post-traumatic stress disorder did not exist in those days, and there was no guidance on how to transition back into society; no warm embrace, no counseling, and no job training. People like my uncle put their bodies, minds, and spirits in the line of fire for a nation they believed in but returned home to the same hatred, racism, and disrespect that existed before they left.

Nobody cared that my uncle had fought so hard and sacrificed so much. Everyone was eager to get back to their lives after the war, forgetting that some had no life to return to.

After a year, Uncle Albert started his own construction company, fixing roofs, gutters, and shingles, and we saw a definite change in him as his business grew. He stood taller and straighter, and we heard his laughter again. Sharing a room with him made me feel like I could really trust him. I would tell him about Mama and Daddy and how Yvonne and I couldn't stand their fighting. One night, after I complained once again about my family, he put his hand on my shoulder, looked me in my eyes, and said, "Wait until you go through what they go through every day out there in this cold, white world. They are not perfect, but they love you. I hear them shout, scream, curse, and push each other around, but that is because they are in pain and they don't know anywhere else to release it. But they're feeding you, right? You got a roof over your head, right? They're putting clothes on your back, right? Why do you think they're doing that? They are doing it because they love you. They ain't perfect."

Uncle Albert had those stare-down army eyes. He didn't stare at me; he stared *through* me, peering directly into my soul. He didn't speak loudly, but I felt every word.

Uncle Eddie, my father's younger brother, was another occupant of Dukie Duke's room. My aunt, Uncle Eddie's wife, had called my father and simply said, "He's dying. Come and get him." Uncle Eddie loved alcohol and drugs beyond anything else. He was always considered the pretty boy with a sense of humor. He was the comedian who could dance well and had a voice like Nat King Cole. Everybody loved his talent. He tried to make it in the entertainment world, but he was crushed by rejection after rejection. To kill the pain, he drank and drugged and drugged and drank until that rainy Saturday morning when my aunt called. Daddy drove me and Uncle Lee from Poughkeepsie to New York City, up the Taconic Parkway in the family DeSoto. On the way, I stared out the window as purple and brown leaves danced their way to the ground. The endless beauty gave me a panoramic view through God's paintbrush.

We found the Harlem address and climbed four flights of creaky stairs. There was no light except the glow of the upper stairwell and the daylight beyond the glass door behind us. We knocked on the door of 5C. Then we knocked harder. Finally, the lock clicked, a latch sprung, and the door cracked open. There stood Uncle Eddie's wife with disheveled hair and tortured eyes. She said in a gravelly voice, "Come in." There was no furniture except for three wooden chairs, one with a large crack down the back. She invited us to sit down but my father shook his head. "Where is he?"

"I know he don't want you to see him like this, but he's in there." She pointed to the small bedroom to the left. Daddy told me to stay put as he and Uncle Lee walked into the bedroom. After a few minutes, I walked over and peeked in the room. Daddy and Uncle Lee were talking in whispers as I looked down and saw Uncle Eddie lying naked on a dirty old mattress. He was about six feet tall, but I was shocked to see that he was skin and bones, maybe no more than one hundred pounds.

Uncle Lee found some clothes to put on Uncle Eddie and stuffed the rest of them in an old suitcase. Daddy lifted Uncle Eddie in his arms and headed out of the room. I opened the door to the hallway and when I looked back, I saw Uncle Eddie's wife kiss Daddy on his cheek and whisper, "Thank you. I love him." As we descended the stairs, Uncle Eddie started crying and repeating how sorry he was. Then Daddy drove home and I sat in the passenger seat while Uncle Lee held Uncle Eddie in his lap. Aside from the wind whistling through a cracked window in the back, it was silent on the ride back to Poughkeepsie. When we arrived home, Uncle Lee and my father put Uncle Eddie in a bathtub and scrubbed him down. Then there was a new occupant in Dukie Duke's room.

There was no mistaking that Uncle Eddie was an addict. I think his frustration was based on the fact that he had enormous talent that was never acknowledged. That caused a lot of soul-searching for me because I had started dreaming about possibly becoming an actor like the ones in those oversized images we watched at the movies. Uncle Eddie was the only person I knew who had an interest in the arts, and I could see that he had talent. I couldn't understand why no one had given him a chance. How frustrating that must have been. After he came to stay with us, whenever I talked about acting, one of my parents would say, "You don't want to end up like your Uncle Eddie, do you?"

Having a new roommate wasn't so bad because we shared an interest in performing. Uncle Eddie could sing, dance, and tell jokes. He would always make me laugh and I could see that he had a big heart and a big spirit. I could also see that he was battling the demons of addiction. I realized drugs and alcohol were the way Uncle Eddie chose to numb the pain of rejection that came with seeing successful performers who were no more talented than he was. He would never get a chance and it was difficult for him to accept that.

I'm sure my parents hoped that his tales of show business frustration would cause me to reexamine my career goals, but the exact opposite happened. I couldn't get enough of his stories, no matter how harrowing. We sat on our beds, and he told me about New York City, how tough you had to be to live there, and how Harlem was no joke. He told me about being a black man in America. "You young now, boy, but you ain't seen nothing yet. Wait until your ass grows up. You're tall and they're going to tell you there ain't no place for a tall, dark-skinned man in America, except prison, but don't believe them. You've got something. I don't know what it is, but I can see it in your eyes." Then he went back to humming and laughing and squeezing my shoulder to let me know he believed in me.

Uncle Eddie stayed with us for a year or more. He did not drink or take drugs that I knew of because my dad and my uncles told him they'd "beat his ass" if he did. One day, Uncle Eddie suddenly packed his bags, gave everyone a big hug, and moved back to New York City to continue following his dream. He said he would write us when he and his wife got settled in a new space. Months went by without a letter. His phone had been disconnected and we had no way to contact him. Everybody was worried about Uncle Eddie. A year later, we got a call from his weeping wife telling us that Uncle Eddie was dead. My father and uncles went to Uncle Eddie's funeral service in New York City but spared us the pain of attending.

I had barely got used to having my own room again when Uncle Howard, my mother's brother, moved in after his divorce. He had been in the U.S. Navy and was always in trouble because he couldn't stand "the white man's disrespect." Uncle Howard had one of the hottest tempers I had ever witnessed. He would snap quickly over the smallest things. *Why are you looking at me so long? What did you mean by that? Do you think I'm stupid?*

Uncle Howard didn't talk to me very much, but he did spend countless hours muttering to himself about things he regretted and how he was never going to allow anybody to disrespect him. He was a master of monologues and self-reflection. He could literally talk to himself for hours in Dukie

Duke's room. I would lie there in silence. When he caught me looking at him he would say, "Boy, what are you lookin' at? You got something to say?" I struggled to stay awake, just waiting for him to fall silent so I could remove the burning cigarette from his hand and put it out in the over-flowing ashtray. I was relieved when he finally remarried and moved out. I just hoped for her sake that he learned to control the anger and frustration he felt as a black man in America.

My father helped find him a job at the De Laval Separating Company, where Uncle Howard worked in the rubber processing sector. My father would invite him over for Friday night fights and the two became very close, debating everything from boxing to politics. My father was an avid reader. He read the newspaper every day. When he disagreed with Uncle Howard, Daddy would cite the newspaper where he got his information. Uncle Howard would get up, tell my father that he shouldn't believe every-thing the white racist man wrote, and say my father and the racist writers could all go to hell. Then he would storm out of the house, slamming the door behind him. This brought uncontrollable laughter each time because my father loved getting under his skin. Uncle Howard would come back the next Friday, and they would do it all over again.

COUSIN ERNEST'S TEETH

The last roommate I had as a teen was Cousin Ernest. He was a nice change because he didn't talk much; he was more of a listener. He moved into Dukie Duke's room after separating from his wife of many years. Cousin Ernest only spoke when he felt he had something of relevance to say. He had a lighter complexion and was teased by the darker family members. He was called things like "high yella" and "half white." When they were finished with their insults, he would respond with a single poignant phrase: "Hell is too good for you." Cousin Ernest was very handy around the house. He could fix almost anything.

One of the things that was upsetting about Cousin Ernest staying in my room was that he would pull out his own teeth, which reminded me of the dentures in Grandma's jar. He did not have health insurance or money to pay for a dentist, so after suffering for days and weeks with a toothache, he'd buy a bottle of whiskey, drink half of it, go to the mirror, pull out his switchblade, sterilize it with alcohol, and slowly but aggressively cut the gums from around his tooth.

I could hear the moans and grunts from the bathroom as he practiced his own form of dentistry. Then he came out of the bathroom, tied one end of a string tightly around the tooth, and the other end of the string to the doorknob. After another drink, he slammed the door shut, snapping the tooth from his mouth. Then he fell asleep. When he woke up, he went to the mirror and examined his handiwork. I witnessed this several times with the same knife and the same gums; only the tooth was different.

One day I made a mistake of lying in bed in pain. I was moaning, and Cousin Ernest asked me what was wrong. I told him I had a toothache. He graciously offered to take care of it for me, but I quickly told him no thank you. I think I hurt his feelings, but if I had a choice of being in pain or suffering the techniques of Cousin Ernest the dentist, I preferred the pain. The next day, Cousin Ernest asked how I felt and I told him my parents had taken me to the dentist. "That's a waste of money," he hissed.

As a young man, I learned how to listen from Cousin Ernest and also how to hear other people, a technique I utilized extensively as an actor. The best performances of my career have been based not only on what I said, but how well I listened to the other actors. Listening is the foundation of acting because it's not what you say as an actor, it's how you respond based upon what you've experienced.

It's interesting how my rotating roster of roommates taught me so many important life lessons. I learned a lot from my parents, but as these men came into my life, they shared life experiences from beyond the Poughkeepsie city limits. I heard stories about how they had dealt with the challenges they faced as black men in a white America. I was fascinated and scared at the same time. I often thought about how different things would be when I moved out on my own. After listening to the struggles these men faced, it made me realize that things would not be easy. However, that fear only fueled my dreams even more. I knew that it wouldn't be easy, but I also realized I had to try. I still wanted to be an actor, but first I had to finish high school.

MAMA'S KITCHEN

Let me tell you something chil'
A fool
Is a fool
Now don't you ever get so grown you forget that
You kids lucky
You got an education
Don't have to go round
Scrubbing somebodies else's floors
You get home
An
Your own dirty
Get yourself an education
Get a job
An make yourself some money
Make something out yourself
Be somebody
Don't be fools
Like
Me an your father
See
We didn't have the chance you kids got
We had to work
An I mean work hard brother
You kids come up stupid its your own fault
But
You do it over my dead body
I kill you before I see you all turn out bums
I ain't worked and slaved
All these years
Washin
These white folks' shit for nothing.
I kill both of you all
And

I mean it
If you all turn out to be bums
You all better not let me hear 'bout it
Cause
I'll find ya
Take a knife an
Cut both you all's throats
Hand me that sugar baby

▪————————————▪

Chapter 5

POETIC LICENSE

If you have a good friend, you don't need a mirror.—German proverb

ROOSEVELT HIGH SCHOOL WAS A LIFE-CHANGING experience. For starters, there were only twelve to fifteen black students in a population numbering in the hundreds. I went to Roosevelt expecting the same kind of anger and defensiveness from elementary and junior high, but I was wrong. I met friends who befriended me without judgment. Dick Check was one of my best friends. He was white, but he never saw color. He treated me with respect, compassion, and humor. Dick introduced me to his friends at Roosevelt, and it quickly became like a brotherhood: If anybody messed with Dick and his friends, I was there to help and defend. If anybody messed with me, Dick and his friends came running. We soon formed a band called Cool Breeze, even though none of us was either cool or good musicians. We just *wanted* to be cool. Dick played the bass and I played the saxophone. Our uniform consisted of long black Bermuda shorts, white socks, black shoes, white button-up shirts, and big black sunglasses. We played one of our first gigs at the end of a school assembly, and to our surprise, the audience applauded. It only encouraged us to play more.

I was on the basketball and football teams but wasn't very good at either. The star of both teams was a friend named Robbie Williams, who later went on to become an undercover agent for the CIA. Robbie was a great athlete. He got injured during a basketball game in the middle of the season and the coach put me in. I don't fully understand what happened after that point, but I know for sure that God has a sense of humor. We were down by about fifteen points at the time, and I came in and started firing up jumpers, which was not one of my strengths. I got the ball six times, and each time I scored! It felt amazing. Robbie came back in the game soon after. Excited by what he had seen, he passed me the ball three times—and I missed all three. The coach took me out and we lost the game. Those six shots were the only points I scored the entire season.

In football, I played defensive tackle and took all my anger and frustration out on the people I tackled. I wasn't a great player, but it was hard for running backs to get past me because of my size. During one game at the end of the season, at kickoff, I was running toward the player with the ball and focused on smashing him to the ground when suddenly, I was hit high and low by a pair of opponents. I passed out immediately and was carried off the field in a stretcher. I never played high school football again.

High school is a time of discovery for most teens, and I was no different. I was an introvert and not well-spoken. I could make people laugh and they liked me for that, but I was missing self-confidence. When I felt frustrated, I'd write my feelings in poems in my journal. My English teacher, Ms. Jean Walker, sincerely cared about her students. She introduced us to the writings of famous authors from around the world and gave us an appreciation for English as a language, but during her class, I was always preoccupied with writing in my journal. Ms. Walker paced the classroom as she taught, looking at each student to make sure they understood what she was saying. She frowned whenever she passed by me, looked at what I was writing, and saw it had nothing to do with what she was teaching. She warned me three times that if I continued doing this, she would take action.

Weeks went by without me writing in my journal during Ms. Walker's class. However, one day at the end of the semester, I came up with a poem idea and I wanted to write it down before I forgot it. Ms. Walker passed by my desk and saw that I was writing. She took my journal from me. I stood up to confront her, but in the strongest and quietest way, she told me to sit down. When class ended, I approached her and asked for my journal back. She said no. I looked at her and told her that I never liked her. She looked back at me and stated that she appreciated that.

My first day back after the break, as I was leaving English class, Ms. Walker said, "Duke, come here." She handed me a wrapped package with a card. "Open it," she said. The card said "Congratulations." I opened the package and it was a book. Inside the book was a list of the winners from the state poetry competition. Ms. Walker had entered my poems in the competition and I was one of the winners. I was in shock, because after she took my journal, I thought she was upset with me and I hated her for that. When I realized what she had done and saw the faith she had in me, I was dumbfounded.

As I stood in silence, she looked at me asked, "What do you think?"

Close to tears, I looked her in her eyes and said, "Thank you, Ms. Walker. You have no idea what this means to me."

"No, Mr. Duke. You have no idea what this means to me."

It was the first time I felt respect and kindness from an adult who was not a relative. Not only that, she was white. That moment changed my life because until that point, my writing had value only to me. Having other people see value in my poetry and award me for what I had written confirmed that I had value and worth. I would never forget what she said to me. "You're talented. You deserved it. Never stop writing."

When I was seventeen, I got a job at a summer camp as a lifeguard, but I did not know how to swim. Still, everything went smoothly until the middle of the summer. I used to take a boat out to the little dock that I sat on, but one day there was a thunderstorm and the boat wasn't available because it was across the pond. It was thundering and lightning and I was just sitting there. Somebody yelled out, "Swim to shore!" I didn't want to lose my job so I jumped in the water. I actually got about fifteen feet before I remembered that I really couldn't swim. At that moment, I went under once, then twice, then I saw my life flash before my eyes. I saw my childhood and everything I had been through while I was sinking and coming up for the last time. I saw my sister, my relatives, and all my experiences before a young girl grabbed me by the neck and pulled me to safety. As I lay there like a pathetic beached whale, the lady who ran the camp stood over me with a scowl. "What happened?" I just looked at her with nothing to say. "Get out."

I realized that going forward I needed to be true to myself and honest about my abilities. If I couldn't do something, I either needed to learn how or be able to admit my shortcomings. Pretending I was something that I wasn't didn't end well for me that day, and maybe that was a sign. Nearly drowning as a lifeguard was humiliating but it spoke to my internal worth. I had only taken the job for the money, and that put people in danger. Something truly horrible could have happened and it would have been my fault. I felt ashamed, but I learned that I was no longer a kid who could get away with things. My actions affected others and I needed to be honest with them and myself.

REBELS

One Saturday evening, my best friend Jake, Yvonne, Robbie, and I decided to go for a ride in the country. We were driving, laughing, and having a good time when we suddenly realized we were lost, so we stopped by a countryside diner. The parking lot was full of pickup trucks with rifles mounted in the back windows. It didn't seem like the best place to stop, but we were desperate. We entered the diner and sat in a booth. The waitress took her time getting to us and seemed agitated. We ordered, but I could sense that we were not welcome. I lost my appetite but I wanted to hear some music so I went to the jukebox, put in a quarter, and chose two songs. I sat back down and started listening. A large white man looked at me, went over to the jukebox, and yanked the cord out of the wall. My friends looked at me and then looked at the white man.

Yvonne grabbed my arm as I got up. "Don't do it." I pulled away from her, went over to the jukebox, plugged it back in, and reselected the song that was playing. I sat back down. The white man looked in my direction again, got back up, went to the jukebox, and turned it off again. This time my sister was adamant. "Let's go!" I got back up, put two more quarters in the jukebox, and chose four songs. The white man stood up again, but this time his wife grabbed him by the shoulder and asked him to sit down. One of the greatest moments in my life was watching that white man's face while the songs that I had chosen played for everyone to hear. After the songs ended, we got up, exited the diner, and got in the car. The white man stood at the door and watched us drive away.

While I was attending Dutchess Community College, my friends and I were very frustrated about the racism we experienced in our hometown of

Poughkeepsie. Our parents encouraged us to move past it, get an education, and do better than those who hated us, but in my twenties, I discovered rebellion within myself. I hung with people who had similar feelings and thoughts. There was a nightclub called Williams and it was known as an all-white club. On the weekends, young white kids went there to drink, party, eat, and have a good time, but no blacks went to Williams. We knew we wouldn't be welcome. One Saturday, Yvonne and I, two of our black friends, and two of our white friends drove to Williams. We took deep breaths and walked through the front door. A live band was playing and everybody was drinking, dancing, and laughing.

Once we saw the joy on the dance floor, we joined in. I could feel the tension in the room, but that didn't bother me until I realized that everyone had gradually left the dance floor and returned to their seats. We kept dancing until the band stopped mid-song. Silence filled the room. The bandleader stared at us and then whispered to his pianist. The band started playing a song that we were all too familiar with. It was called "Bye Bye Blackbird." As they stared at us and played the song, everyone began singing along. Amid the growing hostility, we all decided to leave.

Our anger sparked a discussion that grew into a plan. One of my white friends knew a reporter at the *Poughkeepsie Journal*. We wanted everyone to know what had happened to us. I wrote an article detailing the events that occurred at Williams: the hostility, the mocking, and the pain that we felt at being treated that way. My friend submitted the article to the reporter at the newspaper. They published the article the following week. My friends, teachers, and family tried to comfort us when they read about how we had been treated. We decided to go back to Williams that Saturday. We dressed up, got in our cars with more friends than we had the first time, and entered the nightclub. Just then, the owner approached us and said there must have been some misunderstanding. He welcomed us to the club with open arms, bought us all drinks, and encouraged us to dance. He told us to come back any time. The party really started when we left Williams that night, because we celebrated the victory not only for ourselves but also for any person of color who could now enjoy Williams without the threat of intimidation. It was empowering to create an actual change in behavior, and that feeling stayed with me for a long time.

MY FIRST ACTING

At Dutchess, I had the great fortune of meeting a wonderful woman named Constance Kuhn. She was the head of the Department of Drama and Speech and had a generous heart and an understanding of acting.

In the reading classes in junior high school, we had three levels of readers: eagles, bears, and donkeys. I was a donkey—the lowest reading level—because I was dyslexic at a time when no one knew what that was. To make up for my challenges, I memorized most of *Roget's Thesaurus* because I wanted to appear intelligent. The thesaurus helped me to use big words and synonyms in everyday conversation. When I threw out a big word, my friends looked at me like, *what the hell does that mean?* I wanted to impress people with my vocabulary and let them know I wasn't stupid. Once a student was classified as a donkey, things rarely changed. A donkey rarely moved up to an eagle because the student not only accepted their rating, but others did, too. Even though I read the thesaurus and could write a great portion of it, when it came to reading, I was still a donkey. When Mrs. Kuhn asked me to read a speech in class, I told her I had reading problems. I was a donkey. She said, "You're a bright young man, you'll get over that."

Mrs. Kuhn gave me my first acting experience in Eugene O'Neill's *The Emperor Jones*. When I told her that I had never acted before and I didn't know what to do, she advised me simply to memorize the lines and say them to the character that I was speaking to, listen for my cues, and respond. I had no idea what she was talking about, and she had to break things down for me several times. Something eventually clicked with me, though, and she insisted that I star in the play. It took me days to read *The Emperor Jones*, and a week or more to really understand it because I read one word at a time. I had to put the sentences together in my head to make sense of it.

We had rehearsal a week or two after I read the play, but I had many questions for Mrs. Kuhn. She broke down the meaning of my character, what he was saying, and how I should respond. Mrs. Kuhn even explained the concept of acting to me; what an actor was, what an actor did, and what role theater played in all of that. She saw me as a relevant human being who had talent he didn't know he had, and she was willing to help me explore my potential. She recognized something in me that I did not recognize in myself, which is the sign of a true teacher. She patiently guided me through rehearsals.

I was terrified on opening night because my parents, family, friends, and classmates were in the audience, and it felt like I was being judged. I got stage fright and Mrs. Kuhn actually had to push me onto the stage. I froze for a moment, struck dumb out there, in front of everyone, I stood motionless. My fellow actor repeated his lines a couple of times, and I finally responded with my line. At the end of the play, the curtain went down and then raised again to reveal the audience's standing ovation. I had never experienced anything like that moment and somehow it validated me. It was the first time in my life that anyone had shown that kind of regard for me and my talent. I was in shock and didn't know how to respond.

Although I know I bowed awkwardly, Mrs. Kuhn told me that I bowed perfectly and that was a defining moment in my life. Not just the audience's applause, but the process and the craft of acting that Mrs. Kuhn so graciously took the time to carefully explain to me. I felt something I can't put into words, and it would not go away. It was a blend of pleasure and satisfaction; a feeling of resolve in finding something that I loved and was good at. This was much different from band, football, basketball, or lifeguarding. With those, I was trying to be something that I knew I wasn't. I had wanted to satisfy the expectations of others, and this time I was doing something that felt right to me. I could tell I was meant for acting.

I couldn't wait to hear what my parents thought of my performance. I had been talking about acting for a long time, and they finally got to see me do something I loved. When I got home, sure enough, my parents told me how proud they were. Then Daddy said, "You were really good. I like what you did, but enough of this foolishness. You got to get back to your studies so you can be a doctor." I knew they weren't trying to be mean. They just wanted to protect me from disappointment. There were few major black actors in those days, more or less characters like Stepin Fetchit and Amos 'n' Andy.

After a lot of thought, I gave up my dream and instead tried to follow my parents' instructions. I took classes in anatomy and physiology. I cut up cats and *squalus acanthias* (cape sharks). My bedroom reeked of formaldehyde. Yvonne refused to come into my room after she saw me dissecting cats, squirrels, and frogs. I appreciated the complexity of how bodies were made and was truly fascinated by how they functioned, but I was never meant to be a doctor. I had no passion for it, and it showed when I failed most of my classes. My parents asked me to raise my grades and go to medical school, but I couldn't continue down a path that I knew was not for me.

After days of arguing and weeks of fighting, my mother finally said, "If you hate it that much, you can be a teacher because teachers make money, but you are not dropping out of school. You're always writing in your journal. Be an English teacher." So I applied to several colleges and universities. My girlfriend at the time, Susan, helped me fill out applications and I got scholarship offers through Dr. Martin Luther King Jr. to several schools. I chose to attend Boston University and majored in English as Mama suggested.

Chapter 6

THE AWAKENING

Silence is a source of great strength.—Lao Tzu

I WAS AN INTROVERT TRYING TO pose as an extrovert in college. I did not have a lot of self-confidence or self-worth, but I was starting to grow into my own. I began to learn how to approach young women. Before I turned nineteen, a girl would have to approach me because I had no understanding of how to approach them. My friends teased me about that. I thought maybe the mean things people said were right; maybe I wasn't an attractive young man. Maybe I was too tall, too introverted; maybe I wasn't a smooth talker, smart enough, clever enough.

At church one Sunday, I saw a beautiful young lady named Pat. From the moment I saw her, I knew I cared for her. Our families introduced us because my mother and father knew her parents. I shook her hand, said hello, and complimented her. She smiled and suggested that I call her sometime. She wrote down her number on a piece of paper and I carefully folded it to place in my pocket.

A few days passed. I learned that Pat was visiting her parents in Poughkeepsie for the summer and was going to school at a historically black college. I finally worked up the courage to call her and we decided to go for a ride. I borrowed my mother's car. The first time we went out, she asked about me, and I liked that because she didn't talk much about herself. She asked me who I was and what I was going to do with my life. To be honest, I was getting ready to go to school to study English, but I had no passion. I couldn't talk to her passionately about anything. I just let her know that I was not going to be a dropout and that I valued education, especially because of my family's expectations. She said the same about her family and that she had to go to school or she would've gotten her butt kicked by her mom. I understood her, and we laughed. We laughed about our parents and their discipline of us and our reluctance to obey them. She said she thought I was handsome and kind. I asked her with a trembling breath if she would like to go out again one evening.

A week later, I borrowed my mom's car again and we went to a drive-in movie. It was our second date and I don't even remember the movie we watched because she was the movie I wanted to see. We talked the entire time and then she reached out and held my hand. I looked at her and she leaned over and kissed me on the cheek. I kissed her on her cheek and then we kissed on the lips. That was a pivotal moment for me because I never believed a woman that beautiful could be attracted to me, Bill "Dukie" Duke. I drove her home and we talked the next day on the phone. I took her out a third time, and on this date, I touched her breast. We did not have sex because she said it was too soon and wanted to get to know me better. I agreed, and we kissed goodnight.

The next day she left to go back to school. I was brokenhearted because it was the first time I had felt so deeply for a woman aside from Nancy Wilson, a singer who was on the Cannonball Adderley album cover. Every time I saw her, I wished I could marry her. Other than that, I had never felt for a woman in that way. So I let Pat know that I cared about her in a letter. I asked if I could visit her at college. A week went by with no response. I called her and she said yes to my visit and that she would like to see me. She reiterated that she thought I was handsome and she loved that I was so tall. I started saving money from working and cleaning offices at IBM with my uncles. After a few weeks, I had enough money to buy two new shirts and a bus ticket from Poughkeepsie, New York, to Washington, D.C.

When I arrived, I checked into a room at the run-down motel near her college. The next day, I called her but didn't get an answer. I called again but still didn't get a hold of her. She told me before I came that she wanted to meet me in front of the commissary in the afternoon. I called her another four or five times but still nothing. I wanted to see Pat and wanted her to see me in my new suit, even though it was a bit small for me. The pants were a little short and my jacket sleeves ended too soon, but I put cufflinks on so that it would look like I had purposely shortened them. I had combed my hair and brushed my teeth several times so my breath would not smell bad. At the motel, I asked how to get to the school. I couldn't afford a cab and didn't know how the buses ran, so I walked the three miles to campus. I walked over to the commissary but didn't see her. So I walked all the way back to my motel, depressed and humiliated.

The next day I went back to the commissary and waited for hours. As I was getting ready to leave, I saw her walking by with her friends. I couldn't believe it! I had finally found her! I walked over to her and said "Pat!"

"Oh, there you are," she said casually. "I was wondering where you were."

I explained that I had called her several times but didn't get an answer. As I was talking, her friends were staring at me. She introduced me to her friends and one was a boy named Ron. Ron just looked at me. We shook hands, but he still didn't say anything. I noticed that when they were walking over, Ron had his hand on her shoulder. I stood there uncomfortably until she finally said, "Let's talk."

We sat on a nearby bench. I asked how she was and she said, "I've been busy working and studying."

I said, "We talked about me coming to see you and spending time together."

She said, "I'm so sorry you came down because I'm not going to be able to spend time with you."

"Well, why didn't you just tell me that?" She blamed it on being overwhelmed and busy. I asked, "Are you going to be busy for the next two days?"

She claimed that she had a test and if she didn't get a good grade, her mother would kill her. She apologized again then walked back to her friends. They started talking and a couple of her friends looked over at me and laughed. As they walked away, Ron turned around, stared at me, and slowly put his arm on Pat's shoulder.

I had written letters and poems to Pat and she had written back to me saying how sweet she thought I was and that she had never been treated so well by a young man before. She said she respected me and cared for me, but at that moment, I knew that Ron was the reason she did not call me like I wished she had.

I walked three miles back to the dingy motel and sat on the bed for hours. I didn't even know where I was. I think I was trying to find a way to deal with my feelings of pain, depression, and anger. I felt like I a fool.

Why would she do this to me? What is her problem? Am I not good enough? I knew her skin was lighter and so was Ron's. I was dark, and I wondered if that was the reason. *Was she embarrassed that I was dark?* Many thoughts went through my mind, my soul, and my spirit. They were thoughts that I couldn't totally explain.

The way Pat looked at me at the drive-in movie was so caring and tender. It was the look of future, potential that we could be together someday. It was a softness I had never felt before from any female. I remembered the kindness in her eyes, but the eyes that met me on the campus of Howard University were not the same. I realized it was the look of indifference. She was kind in her dismissal, but her eyes betrayed her words. I knew that I would never see her again. She had betrayed my trust in a way that I could never forgive. When she returned to school and her friends, somehow it reminded her of the great mistake that she had made by giving me mixed signals. She didn't have the courage to say how she truly felt. She didn't have courage or integrity that would have made things easier for me. She just thought that if I came down, she would ignore the fact that I was there and soon I would leave. It felt horrible.

I laid back on the musty bed and started to cry. It started as a little weep but turned into sobbing pain. I cried so deeply and so hard that I fell asleep. I woke up the next morning and got on the bus back to Poughkeepsie. As I looked out the window on the ride back, I felt myself resenting every woman we passed. I also felt the same toward the ladies on the bus. When one of them looked at me or smiled, I thought they hated me and that this was what women did to men. It impacted my trust of women, their words, and their sincerity. I was bitter and felt going forward that if I didn't take advantage of women, they would take advantage of me. They would hurt me, lie to me, and not have compassion for who I was.

If I didn't want to be hurt continually for the rest of my life, I had to always be suspect and realize that whatever they said, I could not trust them. I had to be the one that ended things, not the other way around. It's not that I did not have sex with women or that I didn't kiss them, hold them, or love them on a certain level. I just felt like I was foolish to trust them because I always got hurt. It was easier for me to make those generalizations than to admit to myself that maybe it was something I had done as well. It was a long bus ride, but by the time the bus arrived back at the

Greyhound station in Poughkeepsie, things had changed. I closed my heart that day. The Bill who remained was not the same. That moment would have an everlasting impact on my interactions with women.

By the time I was twenty-five, I thought that the world was mine. I defied everything. I questioned everything, especially death. Does it mean that we are ending or beginning? I'd been taught that this life is just the beginning. It's something that you experience as a spirit in a human body, but you go to heaven and there are angels. God welcomes you and holds you and keeps you forever, amen. However, the weeping at the casket, the loss of feeling, the loss of never seeing loved ones again, the pain, the pulling of bodies from caskets and kissing them, being restrained by ushers screaming. Somehow that contradiction marked my soul and I started thinking and seeing differently. I started wondering. Wondering is not bad, but it leaves you in a space of void. Yes, they are dead, but they are in a better place. Yes, we all die, but we go to a better place. Yes, my weeping and sorrow is a celebration not a contradiction. I went back to church in search of answers and did the best I could.

MY HERO

Cousin Doug was a deacon at the Ebenezer Baptist Church and best friends with the pastor. Cousin Doug was a hero to me and one of the first blacks to work at IBM in Poughkeepsie. He was the best at whatever he took on. He never bragged. He just spoke to you in terms of his accomplishments and you loved him for that because it was a language that you understood. Cousin Doug didn't talk much, choosing instead to walk in his belief, integrity, and faith. As a result, I followed him and loved him, so did Yvonne and other young folks in our family. He had a deep belief in God, the spirit, church, and Jesus.

After church, Cousin Doug's wife always gathered the notes and plans for the next week. Her secretarial duties were profoundly clear, and she did them well. She counted the dollars, put them in a safe place, and kept the church books. Every Sunday, Cousin Doug would take his children home after the service and prepare them for the daily lunch of Sundayness. Then, he'd come back to the church and pick up his wife.

I heard about one unforgettable and undeniably life-changing Sunday when he came back early to pick up his wife and walked in to see the pastor having sex with her on top of a desk. His wife cried in panic and shame. He waited for her to get dressed and as she came toward him, he looked in her eyes and opened the door for her as he always did for women. She walked to the car and he drove her home. They ate the meal that he prepared, and he went on like this for three months, but he never went back to church. He never spoke to his wife during that time, only to the children.

One Sunday, Cousin Doug drove away in his car and was never seen again. To this day we still do not know where he went. We tried the police, investigations—everything—but he never reappeared. Cousin Doug had been my hero and until that Sunday, the church was my hero, too. That event threw everything into question: my faith in religion, pastors, and the church. I didn't understand that kind of betrayal and was too young to digest it. I felt great anger. My parents and I had many conflicts after that because I no longer wanted to go to church, and the more they spoke of forgiveness, the angrier I got. When I looked into Doug's face after that incident, something had drastically changed. There was a void, a numbness in his eyes. I never saw him laugh or smile again. He barely spoke, and he lived a zombie-like existence until that day he drove away. I have never forgotten him.

MEN LIKE ME (PART 2)

Men like me
Were born upstate New York
Raised on hard times, gospel shouts, and pork
When grandpa died it planted all my fear
That anything you love will
Disappear
So we don't let love come too close to me
Thus my feelings melt to mystery
Men like me

Chapter 7

HIGHER LEARNING

*An intellectual is a man who takes more words than necessary
to tell more than he knows.*—Dwight D. Eisenhower

AFTER DUTCHESS COMMUNITY COLLEGE, I WAS fortunate enough to receive
a Martin Luther King Scholarship to Boston University, which meant I
finally had a reason to leave Poughkeepsie. My mother and father thought
my acting dreams were foolish and unrealistic. They had had little education and wanted to make sure my sister and I didn't turn out like them.
They made us go to college because of that, and we didn't have the luxury
of choosing our own majors. I had to take an Old English course at Boston
University in which one of the major topics of the course was Geoffrey
Chaucer. Chaucer was a great writer and great thinker, but I couldn't stay
awake in class. To make things worse, I snored in my sleep. It was that
boring. The second time I was caught falling asleep, my teacher told me if
I fell asleep again, she'd kick me out of the class. I tried, but I fell asleep a
third time and was kicked out as promised. I begged the teacher to let me
stay because I couldn't get my degree without that class. She said no, so I
went back to the dorm.

MY MENTOR

My roommate, Israel, asked what was wrong. When I told him he said,
"Maybe it's a sign. You always talk about your dream of being an actor, but
you haven't had the courage to do it. This might be a perfect time for you

because there is a black man who is the head of the drama department at BU and his name is Mr. Richards." I didn't believe I could get in, but Israel convinced me there was no harm in trying. I had no idea what to use for my audition, so Israel suggested that I use the lines I had memorized from *The Emperor Jones.*

Two or three weeks later, I contacted the department, met Mr. Richards, talked to him for a while, and then auditioned. In the audition, I introduced myself and did my monologue from *The Emperor Jones.* A week later, I was informed that I got into the class, which was a major accomplishment for me. To get into the drama department, you had to take speech, acting, voice, and dance. At the beginning of the semester, I took a ballet class and actually had to wear tights. (I am so glad there was no YouTube at the time.) Some people in the room laughed, but I was trying hard. Bill "Dukie" Duke danced across the floor to classical music in tights. I learned a great deal from Boston University because speech, dance, and voice were things I had never been exposed to. I had no idea there was a craft to acting. I found it to be fascinating and exciting. In Mr. Richard's class, he didn't allow us to just go up and recite some words. We were forced to *become* that person. I had no idea how to do that, but I was learning. He would say "surrender, surrender, surrender" and I had no idea what that meant. He'd say, "There is something larger than your intellect and your ego. There is something in you that is connected to the universe and it knows more than you do about this character. You are the character and always will be the character." I didn't truly understand what he was talking about until after performing several scenes in class.

POT

One day, he would not let me stop until I had fully surrendered. What I realized had happened was that I wasn't just trying to say the lines and be the character anymore. The character had taken over *me.* Prior to this moment, I'd always been taught that the brain, intellect, and mind were the pinnacle of things, but that day I learned that there was something larger and more significant than the brain. There was something big that I could connect with and when that happened, my life changed forever. I'd always been the type to stay orderly and keep things neatly in the box. With help from Mr. Richards's acting experience and other instructors guiding me through speech and movement, I saw things differently for the first time.

After moving out of the dorm, I shared an apartment with two other guys, and across the street lived a young lady I had met in my acting class. Lynn was a white woman with blonde hair who was smart and loved motorcycles. We used to have great conversations about politics, sports, and relationships. When I first met her, she had a boyfriend, but they split up after a couple of months. She invited me to her apartment for her birthday party and I went. Because she was so popular, her apartment was packed with people. I quickly realized that I was the only black guy there. Many asked her who I was, why I was there, and how she knew me. Then everyone started smoking grass—at least I think it was grass. It was something tucked in cigarette- and cigar-sized rollups. I had never taken drugs before or hung out with people who did, but there I was watching people wild out. Bob Dylan, the Beatles, and the Rolling Stones were blasting from the speakers as people danced with reckless abandon and things got crazier. Guys were crawling on the floor and biting girls on the legs as groups of people shouted song lyrics off-key. The room was a blur of dancing with grunts, growls, and screams of passion and pain. There was constant movement.

I felt out of place and I told Lynn, "Thanks for inviting me, but I'm going to head out." She said, "The fun is just beginning. Midnight is when all things start to change. Follow me." She led me to her bedroom and inside there were several people on her bed smoking, drinking, and fondling each other. She ordered them to leave, and after some slurred protests, we were alone. Lynn whipped out a joint, took a puff, and exhaled a cloud of sweet smoke. Then she offered it to me.

"Sorry, I don't do drugs," I said.

"It's medicinal," she countered.

"How?"

"It cures tension, stress, and worries of any kind. So, as a friend, I am passing this along to you. I know we haven't yet, but I really want to sleep with you and taking a puff of this will help me make up my mind in a positive way."

I smiled at Lynn because I liked her. She had a beautiful face and a great body. She had taken the time to talk to me and really listen. Her challenge got my attention and I didn't want to wimp out, so I replied, "Let's do this."

We sat on the end of the bed. She took the first puff and asked me to open my mouth. She blew the smoke from the weed into my lungs. She did that four times. Then, the fifth time, she instructed me take a hit and blow smoke into her mouth. I puffed and blew smoke. I puffed and blew smoke. I puffed and blew smoke. The next time I puffed and blew smoke into her mouth, she kissed me, and that's when things started to go left. When she kissed me, I was sexually aroused, but something threw me on my back on the bed as Bob Dylan's song "All Along the Watchtower" was playing loudly in the background. As I lay there, I saw gigantic arrows coming at me. So I crawled along the bed to escape them, but the arrows stuck into my hands, arms, pelvis, knees, and feet. As Lynn tried to kiss me, I stopped her. "No! You're going to get stuck by the arrows!" She asked what arrows and I replied, "All the arrows stuck in my body. Can't you see?" She told me she couldn't see them and that I would be okay if I just lay down to rest. Then she left the room.

There I was, alone with arrows in me and Bob Dylan singing. I stayed there through several Dylan songs. I fell deeper and deeper and deeper into a dark vacuum of space and time. I don't know how long I was in this void, but when I woke up, Lynn was putting a cold cloth on my forehead. I looked around and everyone was gone. The music had stopped. It was just Lynn and me on the bed, but I was so out of it, I could barely talk. I had never experienced anything like that before in my life. It was hard to even describe. I felt sexually stimulated, but I was afraid to move. I thought I might fall and break into pieces. I felt confusion, but also a sense of pleasure. Lynn asked if I wanted to stay overnight.

I said, "No. I just want to go home because I feel weird."

She replied, "Let me take care of you." She pushed me back on the bed. She started kissing me. When I opened my eyes again, Lynn was looking at me and asked me how I was.

"What happened?" I asked.

She said, "Nothing happened. I was kissing you and you just passed out. I want to apologize. What you smoked last night was really strong. I should've started you off lighter, but I thought since you are so tall that it wouldn't be a problem. Next time, we'll have a better time." I got up and walked to the door. She kissed me good-bye.

My family had always told me never to take drugs because drugs will kill you, but I didn't like to let things beat me, and I felt like marijuana had beat me that night. I wanted to beat marijuana back. So, the next weekend, Lynn invited me over, and for some reason after I smoked that time, food tasted better, I danced longer and harder, until 3:00 in the morning, and Lynn and I had sex until we passed out. It was the start of something I didn't fully understand.

While I was acclimating socially, my time at school looked like it might come to an end. I had received a scholarship to Boston University, but it did not pay for room or board. So, although I had received help, I still needed to work a job to pay for my living expenses. My grades suffered. As a result, I decided to take off a year of school, go back to Poughkeepsie, New York, and return to Boston University when I had enough money saved up for my books, room, and board. That's a lesson I learned from my parents. Work hard for what you want, and never give up.

I thought my parents would understand, but they were disappointed. They wanted to make sure I finished school. While I was home, I went to visit some friends at Dutchess Community College. I ran into Dr. Hall, who was a very strict Navy vet and president of the college at that time. I never liked Dr. Hall because to me he seemed cold and distant. That day, he was coming out of his office and saw me. He called me over and we went into his office and sat down. He said, "I hear you're dropping out of BU." I confirmed this was true and he asked why. I told him that things were going pretty well, but I was struggling because I didn't have enough money to pay for rent and my books, and as a result my grades were going down. He said, "You're not leaving BU."

I insisted that I had to, but he held up his hand to stop me from talking. He reached into his suit and pulled out an envelope. He told me to open it. Inside was a check, and those funds would pay for my books, room, and board at BU for the next two years. I looked at this man, silent. Here was a man who I'd called a "cracker" when telling my family about him, and he was helping me. I said, "What is this?" He told me that he believed in me. To say I was speechless would be an understatement. I had no idea what to do or say. I wanted to cry. It's hard to explain the thoughts going through my head because I was a militant racist at the time. Here was a person I saw as the "white enemy," whom I considered a monster, and he was giving me money for my room and board out of his pocket. It changed my life—I could never again categorize or think of human beings in such broad and general strokes. I now had evidence that not all white people were evil.

Not everybody was inhumane because of their skin color. Not everybody was anything. There are as many bad black people as there are bad white people. Some people are kind. Some people will never change, but some people do change, and I was evidence of that. The concern Dr. Hall demonstrated taught me something about humanity, that it can be evil, but it also can be blissful and beautiful. Seeing other people's humanity expressed through acts of kindness is beyond love. It is a commitment to something I cannot explain.

Thanks to that generosity, I graduated from Boston University. I was focused on acting, but I knew I wasn't ready for Hollywood, so I followed Mr. Lloyd Richards, my mentor, to New York University's Tisch School of the Arts. While at NYU, I met mentors and lifelong friends who would shape my life and career. When I got to New York City, I had no money and no place to live. It was a rough start for what would become some of my most productive years as an up-and-coming actor and director.

My first order of business was to find a job and a place to live. I stayed with a friend that I knew from Boston University. He had a studio apartment with a small kitchen. His place was small, but he said I could stay until I got on my feet. Even though he was struggling, he was gracious enough to allow me to eat the food he had. I got a job at a local supermarket. The real problem was that there was no place to sleep except for the space in a big closet where he kept his clothes. Unfortunately, that was where he kept his cat's litter box. He told me to move the litter box out of the closet so I could sleep in there with Bernie the cat. I placed Bernie's litter box outside the closet door, took my blanket and pillow, lay down on the floor, and fell asleep. Every night as I started to move the litter box, Bernie would meow and growl, showing his teeth. I actually had to talk to the cat. I used to tell Bernie, "I know this is difficult and I know this is your room." Bernie did not want to hear it, and even scratched my legs and arms as I got ready for bed a couple of times. If I kicked him out, he would claw on the door repeatedly, trying to reclaim his rightful spot.

Then I got a cot to sleep on and he'd be sitting on it every day when I got home—sometimes peeing and pooping there if he was feeling especially angry—and I'd grab him by the back of his neck and put him outside the closet while I washed my sheets and pillow. This was the routine for about three months, until I made enough money to get my own place with a friend, and I said good-bye to Bernie. As I was leaving for the last time, Bernie watched me from the closet that he had just regained. I will never forget that as I put my hand on the doorknob, I looked back and Bernie said "*meoooooooooow!*" It was somewhere between the growl of a lion and the meow of a kitty cat, but I interpreted it as Bernie saying, "Thank God your ass is gone."

SURRENDER

Once I was in my own cat-free apartment, I began to focus on my acting at NYU with Mr. Richards and the dean of Tisch School of Arts, Mr. Miller. They were brilliant and well-connected to Broadway and the theater scene in New York. They often talked about the business and industry of acting, discussing resumes and other professional tools I knew nothing about. They gave me a solid understanding of what it meant to be a professional actor and even encouraged me to learn other languages like Spanish and French to help with accents. They taught me how to listen to my body because as the character comes to you, something happens to your body. The character speaks to you and you have to listen to it. At NYU, I also took up directing because they advised that it was better to know more than just acting in such a difficult industry. I started writing my own plays and directing them. It was the experience of my lifetime, all due to the grace of Mr. Miller, Mr. Richards, and all the great teachers at NYU at the time. I even met one of my best friends for life, Gilbert, who was also an acting student.

Mr. Miller was young, brilliant, and on fire to teach students not only Shakespeare, but also the newest techniques in drama, voice, movement, acting, directing, dance, and more. He was always cutting edge, never looking back and forever seeking ways to revolutionize improvisation. He wanted to challenge us with new ways of telling stories. Whether students were telling stories as writers, actors, or directors, Mr. Miller insisted they find their own voice, perspective, and way of sharing their individuality. He was politically active, but he didn't speak out much. He just acted on his beliefs. Mr. Miller stood up for me one time when I spoke out about my militant points of view. He said that whether he agreed with what I said or not, I had the right to say it. We have stayed in touch all of these years. He is still teaching. Whenever I go to New York, I make time to visit him and his wife.

Lloyd Richards was the first major black director on Broadway with *A Raisin in the Sun,* which received many accolades. It starred actors like Sidney Poitier, Ruby Dee, and so many others. Mr. Richards set the bar high for me and the others. A black man directing a play on Broadway with black performers was unheard of at that time. August Wilson remains one of the great poets of our era, and at Yale University, Mr. Richards taught Wilson about dramatic format, playwriting, and character structure. He was responsible for Wilson's career as a playwright. They were both geniuses, but August Wilson wasn't a playwright until Lloyd Richards showed him the way.

Mr. Richards got me my first job with the Negro Ensemble Company in a play called *Day of Absence*, which examined what would happen in America if all blacks suddenly disappeared. I met Douglas Turner Ward and Robert Hooks, the founders of the Negro Ensemble Company, during this production. The Negro Ensemble Company gave black art a voice in the world and enabled black actors, writers, and producers to tour globally with their productions. I was very lucky to be at NYU during that time, because New York was thriving on Broadway, off-Broadway, and off-off-Broadway. It was a very political time in the late '60s and early '70s with marches, protests, the Black Panther Party, Dr. King, and Malcolm X. I never knew what to do or say when those topics came up, because I attended a school filled with white people who were my friends. We had been told this and that about the white man, so I was conflicted because I didn't want to be an Uncle Tom, but I also didn't want to be labeled a militant.

New York University's Tisch School of the Arts was a life-changing experience. Michael Miller—who had the foresight to put together a team of teachers who were not only skilled but truly ahead of their time—ran the school. Among this group of great teachers was the profoundly talented Jean Erdman, a well-known dance and movement choreographer. Jean Erdman was a principal dancer with the Martha Graham Dance Company for several years before making a name for herself in her award-winning off-Broadway work. In 1972, Jean's choreography for *The Two Gentlemen of Verona* was nominated for a Tony Award.

I was fortunate to have her as my instructor. Mrs. Erdman taught that every movement of the body had meaning. Under her, we learned what movement meant in terms of the character being portrayed and what silence and stillness meant to movement. She taught that movement was a physical expression of emotions and that sometimes movement was parallel to our feelings; other times, it was contradictory.

For example, if a woman witnessed someone hurting her child, she could go into a frenzy and try to punish that individual on the spot; she could scratch, kick, punch, fight, and scream. All of these movements would be an expression of the anger, frustration, and outrage that she felt. She may attack that person, injuring them on the spot, and then carry the child in her arms to a safe environment. Or, she could rush over, pick up the child, and go home, returning during the next two days to observe the person who had hurt her child. On day three, after watching the person pick up her child from school, she could quietly find a way of paying back the injury of her child. Initially she did not confront the abuser. She simply took the protective, loving mother position, but she never forgot who hurt her child and lived out the strategy that revenge was a dish best served cold.

Mrs. Erdman taught us that the body can speak and listen and that every movement has conscious and subconscious meaning. She emphasized that both stillness and silence are powerful. When I left Jean Erdman's class and walked down the hallway, I was more observant of the people who passed by.

Mrs. Erdman was married to one of the most famous writers of her time, Joseph Campbell. He was a genius who studied global mythologies and through years of breaking them down, came up with a formula of common mythologies based on his global research. Mr. Campbell determined that all mythologies are in some way related in terms of their heroes. He even wrote a book entitled *The Hero with a Thousand Faces*, and the formula used in many Hollywood movies, including *Star Wars* and *The Matrix*, was Joseph Campbell's formula. I learned a great deal from his books, especially how to fundamentally tell a story. If viewers don't care about the central character and his or her issues, they may enjoy the action, but nobody will relate to the protagonist. Mr. Campbell gave structure to the hero's journey.

He described the role of the protagonists and antagonists. He described the character arc and the story arc. He instructed students on how to connect with humanity in the audience. Without this connection, motion pictures are empty, with action and music but no heart or relevant meaning. He was a genius at describing structurally what any human being faces when deciding to accomplish something.

When I realized that Jean Erdman was married to Joseph Campbell, I asked if she could arrange a meeting for me to sit down with him and talk about the craft of writing. She was able to arrange a meeting in her home in the Village. When I met him, I expected a vivacious, overly confident human being, but I instead met a truly humble spirit. He was a man who loved his wife, his work, and the information he shared with the world. He was open to new ideas and new ways of thinking. He continued to give insight into his work and why he believed what he believed. After a couple of hours of conversation, I thanked Mr. Campbell for his time and insight.

As I was preparing to leave, he asked me to wait a moment. He went back into a room and brought out a small, thin, rectangular wooden box with a turtle carved on the top. He told me it was an ancient box in which medicine men and witch doctors kept healing herbs and scents. He gave me the box and said I should be aware of my culture and its history because his research indicated that the foundation of many societies came from Egypt and other parts of Africa. I was speechless because I knew what it meant to him. We lost contact over the years, but I will never forget that day. I continue to use Joseph Campbell's story and hero structure in all the films I direct. As a writer, he continues to be the foundation of my story arcs and character structure.

During my time at NYU, I was fortunate to also meet Gilbert Moses, a brilliant, talented, handsome, motorcycle-riding, chain-smoking, militant, out-of-control black man. He was one of the founders of the Free Southern Theater, a community theater group with the mission to bring free theater to the South. Free Southern Theater showcased black talent and depicted positive images of African American culture. Establishing something so revolutionary during the 1960s was unheard of, not to mention quite dangerous, but Gilbert was a man who didn't let fear stop him from doing what he wanted to do.

Gilbert also got me my first significant acting job, in an off-Broadway play entitled *Slave Ship* at the Brooklyn Academy of Music. *Slave Ship* was about slaves coming to the Americas and how they were treated during the Middle Passage. A lot of research was done to depict the exact conditions of that ship. It was an experience I still can't forget because they put us on this big platform that had a top, which was the deck of the ship, and the underbelly where the slaves stayed was on rockers so it felt like we were in the water. That was all Gilbert's idea. The ship was packed with half-naked blacks. We had to understand that there were bodies packed into a tight space with unsanitary conditions. Bodies had been tossed overboard, and the slave masters raped the enslaved women. In the midst of starvation and severe dehydration, there were rebellion attempts that led to death. It was something that brought us together not only as a cast, but also as black people. The most remarkable thing about the play was the question of how we survived. How does one survive such inhumanity? It was rumored that the slave ship owners calculated that they would profit if just 60 percent of the slaves survived passage. The conditions meant not all would survive. How did some survive and what did it take?

We had to put ourselves in their position for that play. Those slaves had to sleep shackled in their own filth in darkness and light among other slaves, living *and* dead. They heard echoing screams as carcasses rotted until slave owners felt like throwing them overboard. Maybe once a week they were allowed on deck to breathe fresh air and watch friends jump in the ocean to commit suicide. They'd watch others intentionally run toward a gun and be shot to death so they wouldn't have to endure any longer. Being a part of the *Slave Ship* cast was an enlightening experience. It made me think about the entire journey. While acting in *Slave Ship*, we were put in those conditions on a stage with a rocking boat a couple hundred feet long so we could really experience what it must have been like.

Once slaves reached the destination, they were thrown into dungeon-like castles where families were separated, stacked on one another, and stored in small spaces. The screams, moans, deaths, and rotted carcasses were all things that shook me. After the castles, slaves were shipped to the Americas and Europe, where they were put on auction blocks and sold to the highest bidder. Once they reached the plantations, slaves were whipped and beaten—sometimes killed—out of cruelty and to teach the others a lesson. Slave masters would host "nigger barbeques," during which whites celebrated the hangings and lynching of slaves.

There's a great pictorial book, *Without Sanctuary*, that depicts a celebratory barbeque in which slaves were put on a rotating skewer and burned like pieces of meat. Slave masters also put them in trees with the flame underneath the slaves to dehydrate them. Then they would take pictures with the bodies or the ashes.

Through it all, we survived. We survived the ships, the plantations, and the lynching. After all this inhumane humanity, our people moved on to "freedom," but this word should be taken lightly because Jim Crow and segregation followed. That so-called freedom was not complete because they promised us forty acres and a mule in repayment for their cruelty. My great-grandfather didn't get his; neither did my grandfather or my father and mother. I haven't gotten my forty acres and a mule. They're in debt to us, but they never paid up.

We suffered through it all due to something deep within us, which I call the "alchemist." We took the guts of a pig and turned it into a dish called "chitlins." We took all the stuff they didn't want, like the heels and feet of cows and pigs, and pickled them. We turned everything negative into something positive for our survival. Integration came along socially, but it was nothing close to economic integration. When we were segregated, blacks were forced to deal with one another. We were forced to create our own banks, businesses, and our own Wall Street. It wasn't perfect, but we came together because we had no other choice.

In some ways, I wonder about integration because we were never truly integrated. Financially, we were supposed to find our way, but without a financial foundation, we didn't have much of a chance and to this day we live in an impoverished mentality that we cannot escape. I pray for that to change, but no one is coming to save us. Until we understand that salvation depends on our own self-regard, we are not going to be salvageable and our children will not inherit hope. Black people in this nation have failed one another and I hope that comes to an end. Coming to America on slave ships was the beginning of our survival and journey in America.

Slave Ship was successful, with such great reviews that a European company took us on a tour to Italy and Scandinavia. Two major things happened while we were in Rome. First, we saw the Coliseum. Our tour guide asked us how old the United States of America was. We all stuck our chests out proudly and said a few hundred years old. We were thinking ancient. The tour guide smiled then pointed to a pillar behind us and asked how old we thought the pillar was. He told us it was thousands of years old. It put so much into perspective because there are so many cultures that are much older than ours. They told us about the history of Rome and the history of that Coliseum. It was fascinating to hear about the rituals and ceremonies of another culture. It was an amazing experience that changed my life.

The second experience was one I will never forget. While in Rome, we came out of the hotel and an older lady followed us down the street. When we turned around, she would run away. While we went on a tour, the lady followed us down the street and when we turned around, she ran again. We asked our tour guide why she was following us like that and he went to ask the lady. The tour guide came back laughing. Apparently, the woman was in her seventies. The tour guide said, "You're not gonna believe this, but she said because you're all black people she was looking to see if she could find tails. She couldn't see your tails." We asked what she was talking about. There weren't many black people in Italy at that particular time, and the woman had been told that the coloreds were part monkey and ape.

Each time she followed us, she expected tails to come out of our pant legs and she was always surprised that it didn't happen. We laughed but we were in shock because it was something we'd never heard before. This woman was really looking for tails! Our tour guide told her we didn't have any tails and the lady never followed us again.

Europe was an experience that opened my eyes to so many things in this world that were bigger than Poughkeepsie and even New York City. There was a universe and a world out there that I never experienced before. It was a big deal to get out of Poughkeepsie, but to get out of the country was unimaginable. Being on a plane for so many hours, passports, the food in other countries, the different languages, seeing different people, and understanding different points of view about the world was all new to me. I was very fortunate. After *Slave Ship*, there was no doubt that for the rest of my life I was going to be an actor. I had confidence that I could make a living as an actor from that moment on.

Gilbert Moses was a brilliant director. The second play he directed was *Ain't Supposed to Die a Natural Death*, written by the great Melvin Van

Peebles. Many of the plays by Melvin Van Peebles like *Ain't Supposed to Die a Natural Death* were poems and ideas that he had put together, but Gilbert Moses turned them into plays. *Ain't Supposed to Die a Natural Death* was phenomenal and received several Tony Award nominations.

For a while I was enamored with Minnie Gentry, who played the part of an old woman who warned white people that she'd put a curse on them if they kept blaming bad things on black people. This monologue was entitled, "I Put a Curse on You." I studied acting by watching all the great actors perform onstage, including Minnie Gentry, Barbara Austin, Dick Anthony Williams and his wife Gloria, Clebert Ford, Arthur French, Albert Hall, Garrett Morris, and Beatrice Winde. These were actors many had not heard of at the time, but they were brilliant and a few of them became well-known. They were mentors who looked after me and encouraged me to never give up. They critiqued me when I was onstage and told me how to do it better. They gave me things to aspire to, not by speaking, but by going on that stage and becoming different people during their performances. When I talked to them backstage, I admired their brilliance. One night of the play *Ain't Supposed to Die a Natural Death*, we saw Nina Simone in the audience. Nina Simone was a musical icon, musician, songwriter, and activist who received fifteen Grammy nominations during her career. She mastered the art of music. Listeners didn't just hear her music. They *felt* her music.

Nina was going through a great deal in her life at that time. During one of the speeches, she crawled onstage because Dick Williams, the actor who was playing an abusive cop, was punishing a black woman. Nina came up screaming on the stage, saying "No, no, my husband did that to me; no, no, no, don't do that to her." I think she might have been high on drugs, and the audience in the Ethel Barrymore Theatre was in shock. I guided her offstage and sat her in a chair while she screamed. She calmed down but was still sitting backstage crying after the play was over. Garrett Morris and I walked Nina to her condo across the street from the Lincoln Center and asked for her phone number so that we could check on her. She asked for our phone numbers and addresses. I called Nina a few weeks later to see how she was doing and she said she was okay. She was going through a great deal. We talked for bit and she asked if I could send her some of my poems that she could relate to. After I sent her the poems, I didn't hear from her for weeks, until I received a telegram that said:

I got your poems. They came exactly at the right time. I do not know how you look and I'm not so sure that I want to see you ever, but I think you have saved my life. Thank you Thank you Thank you from my soul

PS Thank you again

Nina Simone

She had apparently forgotten meeting Garrett and I, but I am so glad my poems helped her. Nina Simone was a brave and courageous woman and artist. I will miss her forever.

I graduated from NYU and went with Lloyd to Los Angeles, where he worked on *Gold Watch* for PBS. After he finished, he insisted I stay in L.A. and not return home to New York like I had planned. He said, "You are staying because I believe there is something out here for you." That support and encouragement gave me the career I have today.

Years after, I became Gilbert's assistant on *The Wiz*, and even though Geoffrey Holder got credit for doing little more than putting a clothesline on the stage, Gilbert Moses was the one who did the hard work on *The Wiz*. He was such a talented and brilliant man who left this Earth too soon. He was a great human being and I loved him. He rode his bike and smoked a lot of cigarettes. Unfortunately, years later he passed away from lung cancer. I visited Gilbert at his condo in Silver Lake, California, a few months before his death. He had just been released from the hospital and was resting at home. He greeted me and asked me to join him on the balcony. After we laughed about past experiences, his face became solemn. I asked if he was okay and he informed me that he didn't know how much time he had left. He said that if he had one wish to be fulfilled, it would be to fall in love again: "I love the girlfriend I have now, but I'm not in love with her, and once in love, you never forget the feeling. I just wish I could feel that one more time before I die."

I told him I understood, but up until then, I had never allowed myself the vulnerability to be in love. I had *loved* but had not been *in love*. The words that he spoke on the balcony that day will remain with me forever. He had a positive impact on my life in so many ways. We must never forget the people who came before us. We must understand what they went through during a time when certain freedoms did not exist.

INVISIBLE MAN

This is not the voice
Of a man
Choking down
The flesh of his many disappointments
This is not the voice
Of courage
Upon whom beauty leaves her mark
This is not the voice
Of the future
That cocks its head
Waiting on you
This moment waiting on you
To fulfill your courage
To meet your challenge
This is not the voice of dissent
Beaten into submission
Fearing annihilation
Reciting the basic tenets of survival tactics
History
Has never moved from this moment
History
Clamors like junk in a vagrant's closet
Moments
Collected
Moving noisily upon each other
I am not a prophet
This is not the voice
That prophets use
This voice is a question
Wondering
Wandering
Loosely in the mouth of a dream
Losing light at

The end
Of
His tunnel
Filled
With ghosts of a night gone by
Too soon
An instrument
Plucked
And
Played by the sun
Tuned
By the moon

Chapter 8

A TUMULTUOUS TIME

Every evening I turn my worries over to God.
He's going to be up all night anyway.—Mary C. Crowley

THE '60S WERE A BLUR OF orgasmic fantasy and ecstasy: parties, sex, music, Bob Dylan, the Rolling Stones, Jimi Hendrix, the Beatles, James Brown, Marvin Gaye, the Supremes, Stevie Wonder, Miles Davis, the jazz-blown pipes of John Coltrane, the bass strings of Charlie Mingus, the unapologetic Thelonious Monk, and the Temptations tempting during a feast of carnal existence surrounded by the devastating horror of the Vietnam War. There were baby screams, exploitation, idiocy, madness of greed and conquest, mindless death and blood, loss of limbs and hope, and the deaths of presidents, kings, and courage. It was a time of wandering.

I remember what I don't remember: parties where we slept together in bunches and woke up under a patchwork quilt of understanding sewn together by not quite understanding what happened the night before. We smelled of it, though, and there were stains and spots and sometimes vomited regrets of burns and nosebleeds from snorts and the funk of fading fantasies of nights spent with beautiful women who had lips of love and lust.

The Vietnam War was not going away. I remember a young man standing in front of a tank, the Beatles songs, Bob Dylan songs, and protests. Everything and everyone who could rebel did, and none of us could stand the government's misuse of power. We marched, shouted, and protested in the streets. Many of us went to jail. The Vietnam War started when I was twelve years old and continued into my twenties. They tried to draft me when I graduated high school, but I did not go. I didn't believe in the

Vietnam War and was a conscientious objector. A great musician at the time, Pete Seeger, wrote a letter on my behalf. The letter granted me conscientious objector status and legally kept me out of the service. I refused to go one way or another, but without that letter, I would've gone to jail.

I believed the war was immoral, and that neither President Nixon nor President Johnson had a right to make that war happen. So Pete wrote his letter and I stayed home and attended Dutchess Community College.

There was suffering of a different kind in Poughkeepsie. I wanted to get help for the people I loved who suffered from lack of work. I wanted to know if there was a way to increase the chances of survival for the people I saw suffering on the streets. I hoped that the growing homeless population got some assistance to give them hope, but none of this occurred. Instead, it felt like layers and layers of suffering were piled on those people and they were expected to dig their way out of it.

This was one of the more difficult times in my life because I was also challenged by people who went into the armed forces. I was called a "little punk" for not going. As the war dragged on and more young men were killed, it was heartbreaking because I knew the families of some of the boys who didn't come back. I never really got a clear answer for our reason for going to war. Were the Vietnamese people so deeply threatening that we had to kill them? I didn't know then and still don't know now. Financially, I know the war served a purpose, but morally and ethically it did not. It helped us grow suspicious of each other. Was that a good thing? In my opinion, no.

The '60s were a tumultuous time for many. Although integration was relatively new and constricted, I lived through the '60s freely. It was a time of serial sexual encounters with multiple women. It was a time of free-spiritedness. It was Woodstock, a three-day festival in the summer of 1969, during which hundreds of thousands of people flocked to see the greatest music of the time, stayed overnight, had sex outside, smoked grass, drank liquor, and enjoyed being drunk and high. There, we explored every possibility and every combination. It felt like nothing was left to question, because we basically had tried it all. We used to get so high that we didn't know we were high and felt like there was something wrong with everybody else because we had snorted and smoked "the sight." We knew that we had the insight of the sight of sightlessness, of sight that would give insight to the sight to the sightless and give sight from our oversight that would lead to sight for the sightless. Dig it? If they could only see our sight, the whole world would be at peace. The sightless would see for the first time. The blind would open their eyes to sight that would end the fight and would shine the light forever. Dig it.

It was the freest time in the world until something called herpes came along. Before that, the worst you could get was crabs. When I was a young man, I was most frightened by waking one morning next to an unknown female and finding myself itching the whole day afterward. The doctor I visited picked from my pubic hairs a crawling creature called a crab. I examined its eyes and clinging appendages, overwhelmed by curiosity and panic. I thought I would die because I had never seen a crawling creature called a crab and asked the doctor if it was the end. He assured me the condition was curable. The doctor sprayed my genitals and gave me a cream to apply so the monsters would die. A miracle occurred and the crabby monsters slowly disappeared. I was so happy, but also pissed at the girls I was sleeping with. I didn't know for sure which girl had given it to me, so I was pissed at all of them. I stopped sleeping with that group of ladies and moved on to another one.

Not long after my scare, something happened to stop all of us in our tracks: herpes. Until that time, any sexually transmitted disease you got was curable with antibiotics, and it didn't come back. We could not adjust to herpes. A friend of mine showed me blisters and sores on his lips. He said he had been to the doctor and they told him it was something that was not going away and that it came from the vagina of a beautiful woman he had met for the first time and had trusted. Herpes was the result of his trust. There was no penicillin, no antibiotics, and no cure to make disappear the sores and wounds that had resulted from their evenings of lust. The pain of that moment now that I look back on it was the naivety of an era whose innocence would last forever.

A sexually transmitted disease that could not be cured? We thought there was a mistake, some kind of conspiracy, or that the doctor had made it up to impair our freedom, the messages in the music, our rebellion, and our desire to bring the systems down by jumping in the face of containment.

Everything came into question because of this personal attack on what we called our sexual freedom. It was now restricted by the reality that there were consequences to our relatively irresponsible behavior and made it so that we had to warn our partners if we were afflicted with the disease. When the sores healed and the blisters went away, it did not mean the disease was gone, and from that point we had to use protection from something that we could spread. Our behavior had to change. We couldn't sleep with just anybody; we had to ask questions like, "Have you been to the doctor?" It killed the romance but helped protect us to a certain extent.

Some of us were still dangerous, didn't want to be restricted, and kept sleeping around without protection. Diseases kept spreading. It was a complicated time because you didn't want to give up your freedom, but you really didn't want to contract an incurable disease. So, you were in a constant state of questioning the world and yourself. *Why is this happening to me? Why are people doing this?* They were the whys of the time. Parties lost their luster. Music did not feel the same. Embraces were not as deep. Something was lost. There were questions in the eyes, but little did we know that herpes was bliss compared to what was to come. It was just the beginning.

The freedoms we once had no longer existed. We began to question the world and ourselves because there was no safety in lying down with each other anymore. There were questions about the consequences of this lifestyle. There was always a questioning.

My sexual behavior, for one, completely changed. I was terrified of everybody. I constantly worried that I had something. Did I have something that I didn't know about? I got tested for herpes and thankfully I didn't have it, but what really kicked the wheels off the spoke was the emergence of a new disease. AIDS was the final blow. Herpes couldn't kill you; AIDS was another story. When AIDS emerged, it was disaster time. We didn't know how to deal with it. They told us it came from monkeys in Africa, but how? We couldn't figure that out. We were told there was no treatment available. It was a dark cloud that came into our lives that not only hovered but settled through us and into the ground on which we stood.

I watched my friend Frank die. My girlfriend and I visited his bedside at his home. A man of vibrancy. An actor. A great talent. A man who inspired many with his open heart and understanding, a man whose boyfriend had betrayed him with a secret that he did not share until it was too late. He lay on his couch laughing, telling jokes, and reminding me of the good times we shared. He had shined like a beacon in a play I'd directed. The audience was in awe of his ability to capture their imaginations, touch their hearts, and bring tears to their eyes. He cried that afternoon, in his small, cramped apartment. I feel shame to this day that I shook his hand but did not embrace him. I did not hold him to my heart, comfort him, or let him know that he was loved. I showed compassion but not caring.

It was cowardly love, because back then we were told that AIDS could be spread by touching. I was ashamed because I told him I loved him but did not show it in an era of ignorance and fear. It was a time of social devastation, of death of many friends and loved ones, a time of suspicion, mistrust, anger, rage, and regret. We really didn't understand the magnitude of how our reality had shifted. What we had called "freedom" had turned into suspicion, fear, and paranoia. Words cannot express the harsh truth of the real impact of AIDS at that time, nor can they define the void created by reality as we rose from dust to a different understanding.

HAROLD

My friend Harold Pierson was openly gay. In those days, if you were a man and hung out with a gay man, it was assumed that you were gay, too. I am not gay, but I loved Harold Pierson like a brother. He was one of most generous, kind, funny, openhearted spirits I've ever met. He did not apologize for who he was. Our laughter and love spanned a twenty-year friendship. Harold had an operatic voice and could sing flawlessly, unannounced, to those around him. His life was opera. He was also a master martial artist; a choreographer not only of dance but of life and the relationships around him.

Harold studied the most famous choreographers, from the Alvin Ailey group to other dance groups to ballet. He knew all the kinds of choreography because he was a genius who never wanted to be second best. He had been a dancer, a singer, and a performer who, at a certain age, stopped performing and began to teach other folks those skills. People grew from whatever he was involved in because of his generosity of spirit. Harold was one who didn't just teach the steps, he taught from the meaning of things. It was less about what a dance routine meant and more about what each step meant. Harold taught that every step in a routine has a meaning, a purpose, and a feeling behind it that said, "Hey, you're worthy of this opportunity, but your worthiness is only going to be defined by your execution."

He would always say *better, better, better.* Even the nights of performances he'd say *better, better, better.* And you'd be pissed off at him, but at the same time, every night you would try to be better, better, better, because Harold never stopped saying it. He simply wanted to do and be the best at whatever he did. People respected him and appreciated him for that.

Harold didn't go as far as perhaps he could have because he wasn't a politician. Harold spoke his mind, and his voice was a voice of honesty. One thing everybody knew was that if you don't want the truth, don't ask Harold. He didn't bite his tongue and he didn't apologize for it. He'd say, "if you ask me what I think or feel, I'm going to tell you. You know me, now, so don't come to me with no BS." When I directed something and wanted someone's honest assessment, I would call Harold Pierson. When I was acting in a play and I wanted an honest assessment, I went to Harold. If I was writing and directing something and I wanted to make it better, I would talk to Harold. He was the catalyst for whatever you accomplished that went beyond your expectations. He pushed you into a space you had not been before not only by making you do it over and over again, but by giving you the insight as to why you're doing it over and over again. *Better, better, better.*

Harold helped you to understand that you had to forgive yourself for not being perfect, but you had to work hard in order to get as close as possible. He also taught you to compare yourself only to your potential. He used to say, "your potential is limitless." Harold said that the only things that limit your potential is your perception of yourself, your reality, your abilities, and your willingness—or unwillingness—to continue in spite of pain. By pain he meant physical pain, mental pain, and emotional pain. I learned how to overcome self-doubt from Harold Pierson, and I don't even think he realized that. Whenever I was ready to quit, I would see an older white man's bearded face beaming red and white eyes, looking down at me from the sky and laughing a deep, I-told-you-so laugh. *You're never going to be anything. You're meant to be less than others. You are not going to make it. You've tried so hard and this is proof that not only will you not make it, but you should stop trying and start doing something else more appropriate for your kind.*

I'm not exaggerating. Every time I saw that face and heard that voice, I thought of Harold Pierson saying *okay, you're getting there. Better, better, better. There you go. Just don't stop.* Because of Harold's words, I haven't stopped. I will never stop.

I refute all of those inner voices that put doubt in your mind about your ability to do whatever you love to do, care to do, or want to do. I refute all those little ants in your mind that turn you against yourself, all the horrific thoughts of failure and mediocrity, and all the self-comparison to the greats. I refute putting yourself in the darkness, where the light is too far away, all of the self-doubt that racism puts in your head and thoughts that make you feel consciously and unconsciously not quite as good as the standard because the standard does not look, talk, or think like you. I refute thoughts that the standard is something you can strive for but never achieve, that you'll get credit for striving but never be equal, and you'll never compare to excellence.

I refute all of that. Harold taught me that whether I am recognized or not is irrelevant, what matters is that that I have tried my best to do my best. No matter how many roadblocks I face, I will never forget the golden voice of my friend for life, Harold Pierson.

Not bad. Keep going. It's better. Getting better. Don't stop. Don't give up. It's getting better. Better, better, better.

Harold and I clicked because we had a lot in common. He was judged differently than me but judged nonetheless. I was a big, tall, dark, and some-times bald black man with an imposing figure. He, too, was tall and dark, but instead of threatening, he was considered unacceptable, unwanted, a weirdo, a homo, a fag, and a sissy. Harold and I used to drive from New York City to see my family in Poughkeepsie in summers, springs, winters, and falls, when God's hands had painted trees orange, purple, yellow, green, brown. Trees that reflected the power and beauty of nature mixed with our laughter as we headed north on the Taconic Parkway, the world swirling around us and the music on the radio. James Brown. *Say it loud. I'm black and I'm proud.* Sometimes we'd take the train. Those were always great rides because we had intense conversations about politics, life, relationships, and the pains in our lives. He'd always have something funny to say that was enlightening and insightful, because he was a brilliant human being.

We would arrive in Poughkeepsie just in time to feast on what my mother and sister had prepared: collard greens, biscuits, baked hams, short ribs, sweet potatoes, apple and pumpkin pies, chicken, black-eyed peas, cornbread, cakes, ice cream, Kool-Aid. After every meal, once the laughter and conversations about politics, sports, the future of the black and white races, personal pains and anguish, Dr. King, Muhammad Ali, Joe Frazier, President Kennedy, President Johnson, Bobby Kennedy's death, Malcolm X, Doctor J, the New York Knicks, the Brooklyn Dodgers, Aretha Franklin's latest hits, and Nancy Wilson had died down, Harold Pierson would lie on the floor in the corner of the dining room curled up in a ball of comfort, safety, and surrender, snoring loudly. The noise was so loud we had to turn up the television to watch the news.

My mother and Harold were the best of friends. He was one of my mother's favorite people. I wouldn't say she loved Harold more than me, but she loved him nearly as much as me. If I came up without Harold she'd ask where he was. *How could you come to this house without Harold? That's my other son. Where's Harold?* They loved to laugh together. We never knew about what, but they would laugh together and never tell us why. I remember when my mother was sick, Harold would go in her room, sit with her, and hold her hand. He didn't talk much, but he listened to everything she had to say. We all loved him for that because he was a human being who cared for other human beings. Mama Duke and Yvonne loved Harold Pierson. He was loveable and cared about everybody. He would let you know he cared not by what he said, but by what he did, and if he cared for you, there was nothing he wouldn't do. From helping you wash your laundry or carrying your groceries to listening to the foolishness you'd speak. He listened to the same stories over and over again and laughed with you each time.

Harold choreographed a play written by the great comedian Garrett Morris called *The Secret Place.* Our friend, Obba Babatundé, was in it and I directed it. Harold was supposed to teach the actors a basic song, but he ended up teaching them an opera song that made it into the play. He demonstrated his operatic voice—which was not a voice you wanted to hear often—and we'd tease him, but he would sing anyway, sometimes multiple times, even if the actors said they got it. That was another reason we loved him: he didn't care what anyone thought of him, what was important to him was what he thought of himself.

I vividly remember the turning point in Harold's life. He got off the train one day and was walking to his apartment. He had to go through a park where he was teased and laughed at by a group of young black men because of his feminine swagger. One day, three young black men approached him, surrounding him with hatred and insults. Harold turned to face them. Situations like that were exactly why he was a trained master martial artist. He had to be, after being physically attacked so many times in his life. You simply didn't mess with Harold Pierson because he would kick your ass. These young men had no idea, but Harold simply looked at them and kept walking to avoid confrontation. The men continued to direct their hate speech at Harold and one of them went after him. When he grabbed Harold, Harold said, "Young man, you don't want to do this. I am not bothering you and I don't want to be bothered." The young man called Harold a bitch and told him to shut up. Harold turned away to keep walking, but the young man made a mistake. He swung at Harold.

Harold dodged the punch and knocked the man out with a punch of his own, but the fight drew the other men over. Harold fought them off for a while, but he was outnumbered, and they eventually beat him unconscious. My friend Harold lay on the ground at the park with blood coming from his nose, eyes, and face until someone called an ambulance and he was taken to the hospital. Harold physically recovered after the beating but was never the same Harold after that day in the park. The new Harold wasn't despondent or depressed, but those young men had taken something from him. He couldn't say exactly what it was they took, but he knew it was gone. They beat more than his physical exterior; they beat his heart. They beat his soul. We laughed and went to Poughkeepsie after that, but his laugh was not the same, and a couple years after that beating, Harold died.

His family didn't say how, but I'm sure it had something to do with AIDS, brought on by a broken spirit. After the attack, I asked Harold if I could go back to the park and find those men because I would've made sure they knew what they did was wrong and unforgiveable. He told me no, but I went there anyway. There were no men there that day.

Harold Pierson took a lot of things that we shared with him when he died—laughter, joy, intellectual conversations, mutual confirmations of who we were, social commentary, and our ability to laugh at ourselves. Something deeply anchored to my soul left the day that Harold Pierson died. His death represented the end of a period of freedom for me. Harold was a pioneer, a courageous soul that gave courage to all the souls that surrounded him and that offered a friendship and bonding none of us will forget. He withstood all the critiques and laughter. People asked if Harold loved me and he'd say yes. They'd ask if I loved Harold and I'd say yes. They couldn't understand how Harold—who loved men—and me—who loved women—could be friends but not lovers. People tend to avoid anything that does not fit into their intellectual box, dismissing it with either humor or disdain. Harold is someone I miss to this day. His friendship always will live in my heart and in that of my family, who break into smiles, laughter, and stories the minute his name comes up. Harold Pierson. His spirit still lives with us.

RUBIN (FOR AWINO)

Rubin
Was
Rough
And
Had the scars to prove it
Tip and tongue
Was
Right on time
Smiled in the right places
Cried on cue
Kept to himself
And gave only that
Which he couldn't use
Now days and nights
Are melted blues
And
What has happened
To
Rubin's shoes

Part III

SUCCESS AND FAILURE

As Duane (aka Abdullah) in *Car Wash*, my first feature film role.
Universal Pictures/Photofest © Universal Pictures

Chapter 9

1968—THE DEATH OF COURAGE

A vote is like a rifle; its usefulness depends upon the character of the user.—Theodore Roosevelt

IN 1963, I WAS A DASHIKI-WEARING twenty-year-old full of resistance and protest going back to the roots of my African ancestry. *Ungawa! Black power! No justice, no peace!* It was a time of Fidel Castro, missiles, the Beatles, Bob Dylan, "All along the Watchtower," Peter, Paul, and Mary, Miles Davis, communism, and socialism. A time for change and a time for hope. The devils must go. Rise up. Rise up. Rise up. A time of the youth movement, the Peace Corps, the March on Washington, Dr. King. The Vietnam War, *The Andy Griffith Show*, picket signs, picket lines, Alabama lunch counter sit-ins, civil rights protests with dog bites, water hoses, and police brutality. *All we are saying is give peace a chance.* Medgar Evers dead. JFK dead. Four little girls dead in a church bombing in Birmingham, Alabama. Malcolm dead. Dr. King dead. Robert Kennedy dead. Sam Cooke dead. *A change is gonna come.*

Despite the constant hits to our courage, we kept singing. We were saved from a pool of despair by a voice of hope, reason, and civility; the voice of a King. Medgar Evers was an activist in Mississippi during the most volatile racial climate in Mississippi's history. Mississippi was one of the most violent states for black people with lynching and torture, a place where hot coffee was poured over the faces, heads, and bodies of lunch counter protesters. Medgar Evers never allowed the threats to him and his family stop him from standing up for his rights and the rights of colored people. One night while heading to the door of his home, Evers was shot in the back by Byron De La Beckwith. Evers rose and tried to make it to the front door. His wife and children rushed him to an all-white local hospital in Jackson, Mississippi.

The hospital initially refused to admit him because of his race but relented once they learned who he was. Medgar Evers died later that day, assassinated June 12, 1963. Byron De La Beckwith went to trial twice and both all-white juries resulted with no verdict. He lived as a free man for nearly thirty years until Evers's widow, Myrlie, took the case back to court and Beckwith was found guilty of first-degree murder. He served seven years in prison before dying at the age of eighty.

Medgar Evers, like Dr. King and Malcolm X, is a hero to me not only because of what he had the courage to do, but because of the sacrifices he was willing to make. Each of those three men knew they could die fighting for their rights, but they were willing to put their lives on the line because they refused to live in a society that treated them and their families as less than human. They'd rather be dead and free than alive and enslaved. Evers knew something larger and more important than his individual life was at stake.

John F. Kennedy was not a perfect president, but aided by people like his brother and Dr. King, he became a voice of hope for America on some levels. There was openness to his discussions about racial issues. With advice from his brother Bobby, he seemed to become more involved in issues of war, race, and other significant matters that America faced at that time. JFK was fatally shot on November 22, 1963, by Lee Harvey Oswald during a presidential motorcade in Dallas, Texas, but we kept singing, shouting, and marching.

Despite the cold-hot war, the beating of innocent marchers, and the dog bites, we still marched and we still sang and we still hoped. We still believed that somehow, someday, someone, or something would bring the salvation, the hope, the drying of internal tears inflicted by a magic bullet from Lee Harvey Oswald and its deep red blood spray across the sunlight.

In 1963, we had something taken from us. Something we could not describe. But when the hope of our youth died with the body of President John F. Kennedy, something in us turned not totally to darkness. Anger filled the air, but Dr. King soothed our wounds with the message of peaceful protest. Malcolm told us the chickens had come home to roost, and there were cries of "off with his head." JFK's death crushed the hearts of Americans—not just the white Americans, but the black Americans who believed that his youth and enthusiasm potentially could have led to greater possibilities for the black race.

They all stood for things, up against a system that told them to sit down, but they refused. Their deaths put an end to some of their efforts but brought about the beginning of something else. We took the message seriously: if you stood up for something outside the parameters of the system or challenged the status quo, you could die. Knowledge of those repercussions created a climate of cowardice, fear, resentment, and quiet hostility. The death of John F. Kennedy tilted the ship. We still moved forward; a little more slowly and in pain, but we moved. We were spirited by the voices of Bob Dylan, the Beatles, Miles Davis, Charlie Mingus, Aretha Franklin, the Supremes, Little Richard, and the Temptations. They united us in their music.

Malcolm X was shot more than a dozen times while delivering a speech at the Audubon Ballroom on February 21, 1965, in New York City. I was shocked by his death but not surprised. Standing up and speaking a voice of reason, protest, pride, focused anger, was not tolerated in the face of what had been determined as our destiny.

A piece of us fell to the floor with Malcolm, right next to his bleeding body. I loved Malcolm, as many of us protesters did. We were conflicted; even though he spoke the truth, it was a truth of challenge and that challenge required commitment and revolt. A spokesman for a part of us was gone, slumped to the floor in front of his wife and children, who rushed to his mortally wounded body and held him close until his eyes went blank, taking with him the spirit of something impossible to describe.

Everyone thought those deaths were part of a conspiracy, and there were arguments and discussions about whether the government was involved. No one doubted that they were efforts to shut down protests and spread fear that protesters would pay a severe price. We thought we had seen the worst, but the worst was yet to come. Three years later, on April 4, 1968, Dr. Martin Luther King Jr. was assassinated while standing on the balcony outside of his Lorraine Motel room in Memphis, Tennessee. James Earl Ray was later convicted of his murder.

I'd like to be able to say where I was and what I was doing when I heard of Dr. King's death, but to be truthful, I went numb. My memory—part of my passion, my hope, my promises to my community and myself—went numb. On some levels, I remain numb until this day. I did not watch the parade with Dr. King's body; I turned off my television.

Numbness is beyond pain. At least with pain, you're in touch with feelings. You can locate them, and if they can be located, they can be medicated, but numbness shuts you off from yourself. You no longer know who or where you are. You're there and not there at the same time. Many were in a state of shock, a state of being completely overwhelmed, drained of anger, hope, or caring. I was six feet and five inches of empty blackness.

It's easy to say, "just get over it," but it's difficult—*very* difficult—if you no longer know what to get over. We killed our pain with smokes and snorts of white numbness and various liquors and parties and clubs.

The death of those men—those martyrs—changed this nation and the world. For those of us inspired by the eloquent moments of Dr. King's "I Have a Dream" speech in Washington D.C., that dream became our nightmare. I did not speak for a very long time after that. People would call me and ask me questions: *Why haven't you been in touch? What's wrong with you? How are you doing? Why didn't you call me back? Where are you? What do you need? What do you want?* For a while, I was robbed of the ability to answer those questions. To my surprise, Dr. King's assassination wasn't the end of the heartbreak.

Robert F. Kennedy was a lawyer turned politician who served as the attorney general for his brother, President John F. Kennedy. After his brother's assassination, he ran for U.S. Senate and won. RFK didn't stop there. He ran to become the Democratic nominee for president of the United States, but his journey was cut short. On June 5, 1968, at the Ambassador Hotel in Los Angeles, California, Robert F. Kennedy was fatally shot by Sirhan Sirhan while exiting through the hotel kitchen following a speech. To me, Robert F. Kennedy was the last person to bring a sense of hope to this nation during the 1960s. He consistently spoke of people coming together, not separated by race or political views. While speaking in Indianapolis, RFK informed the world of Dr. King's assassination. His

Me (front row on left) with friends and family, including the Penfield sisters and my sister Yvonne. *From the author's collection*

Playing basketball in high school. *From the author's collection*

Drama Club: my first acting class at Dutchess Community College in Poughkeepsie, New York. Constance Kuhn is seated in the center. *From the author's collection*

Making my acting debut in Eugene O'Neill's *The Emperor Jones*.
From the author's collection

My Broadway debut in Melvin Van Peebles's *Ain't Supposed to Die a Natural Death*, directed by the great Gilbert Moses. *From the author's collection*

With Richard Gere in *American Gigolo* (1980). *Paramount Pictures/Photofest*
© *Paramount Pictures*

On my behalf, my parents accept a graduate recognition award from Dutchess Community College in the early 1980s. *From the author's collection*

With Arnold Schwarzenegger, Elpidia Carrillo, and Carl Weathers in *Predator* (1987).
20th Century Fox/Photofest © 20th Century Fox

Mother and me in the 1980s. *From the author's collection*

My goddaughter Nathalie. *From the author's collection*

On the set of *Deep Cover* (1992) with Jeff Goldblum, Laurence Fishburne, and writer Henry Bean. *From the author's collection*

On the set of *Cemetery Club* (1993) with Diane Ladd, Ellen Burstyn, and my former drama teacher Olympia Dukakis. *Buena Vista Pictures/Photofest © Buena Vista Pictures*

With my good friend, Danny Glover. *From the author's collection*

On the set of *Sister Act 2* (1993) with Whoopi Goldberg. *From the author's collection*

On the set of my first television pilot, *New York Undercover* (1994), with Gladys Knight. *From the author's collection*

On the set of *Hoodlum* (1997) with Laurence Fishburne (far left).
New Line Cinema/Photofest © New Line Cinema

speech suggested unity and compassion as a nation as opposed to hatred and vengeance. RFK stood poised and strong, addressing a hurting nation and its racial divisions.

Something occurred within me and many I knew during this time that is difficult to describe. It was a mixture of rage, sorrow, pain, frustration, resentment, and anger. It was a feeling that made you want to hurt somebody badly; somebody white, somebody who is part of the system, somebody who caused this. Yes, there were some riots and some deaths, but nothing could bring back the hope that had been taken from us. When Bobby Kennedy died, most blacks felt they had lost an ally who would make things better for minorities in this nation and around the world. He did not live long enough to realize that dream. From his death and the deaths of the others, a cloud of hopelessness was created that still hangs over us today.

The coincidence of Dr. King, Malcolm X, and Robert Kennedy being murdered in hotels fed into our paranoia during those uneasy times. It only added to the pain. When I speak of this in this book, I must admit that there's a part of me that still lies dead in the blood of the Kennedys, Malcolm, Medgar, and Martin. No matter how many times those spots have been washed to cleanse the balconies and floors of the hotels where Bobby Kennedy, Malcolm, and Martin were killed, no matter how much bleach was used in John F. Kennedy's car, there are certain stains that can never be removed. I have not gotten over it. I don't think I ever will.

Although they were different in terms of ethnicity, strategy, and philosophy, there was one thing these gentlemen had in common: the courage to speak the truth. When we lost them, we lost some important values. Because of the way they died, many of us were afraid that if we spoke up, we would receive the same treatment. Some of us were made to feel like cowards afraid to speak our own truth, but some of us did not hold back, expressing ourselves through music, politics, sports, and activism. Many have continued to do so. I celebrate those men and their efforts because their courage is needed again in this world. I didn't say in America, but throughout this world. Without the courage of men like that, we may dream, but those dreams may not come true.

FOR MALCOLM

I saw a picture of a man lying on a floor
He was dying, bullet wounds in his chest
And as I stared at the picture I wondered about his life
Deserting him with everybody watching veiled in helplessness
Yes, they called our bluff
We said they wouldn't do it and
We said what we would do if they did it
So they did and we didn't so they killed the King and we didn't
We were too busy figuring out how we could not know what to do
Too busy making money and wanting to be movie stars
Too busy being black and beautiful
Too busy getting high and trying to lose our way
Too busy trying to find thicker lies to tell ourselves
Feeling sorry for ourselves
Lying there he looked like he was trying to say something
Trying to scream something thru his bloody lips and
It wasn't love, it wasn't love

Chapter 10

INSPIRATIONS AND ASPIRATIONS

Fifty percent of something is better than one hundred percent of nothing.—English proverb

THE DEFINITION OF INSPIRATION IS THE process of being mentally stimulated to do something creative. Many have inspired me throughout my life, beginning with my mother and father, and numerous relatives, teachers, and neighbors. They told me never to give up, to follow my dreams, and, even though my parents objected to my unrealistic desire to be in the movie business, they later supported me 1,000 percent. There are people in this life, whether they know it or not, who inspire through their lives, actions, and deeds. They give people who observe their courage the will to get up when they fall.

PIONEERS

Oscar Misheau

Oscar Misheau is one of those people. Born January 2, 1884, Oscar was the first African American filmmaker. His film, *Body and Soul*, marked Paul Robeson's acting debut. Misheau even launched a production company to make his own feature films. His films, mainly labeled "race films," were boldly political and his visions were unmatched. Misheau operated on a by-any-means-necessary mentality, which meant he took matters into his own hands. If there was no funding for his film, he would generate it by selling stocks. If there was no distributor, he'd distribute his own films. He was a one-man show. Before becoming a filmmaker, he was a successful writer. Over the course of nearly thirty years, Misheau wrote seven novels and wrote, produced, and directed forty-four feature films, an achievement viewed as impossible for a black man to accomplish. He persevered against unthinkable odds and gave courage to black visionaries after him.

Oscar Misheau showed all of us how to make a way out of "no way" if you are willing to make the sacrifices to realize your dreams. His life was a statement, and that statement was profoundly simple: never stop. Never give up. Believe in yourself and let no one ever take away your dreams.

Frank Capra

Two films got my attention growing up: *It's a Wonderful Life* and *Mr. Smith Goes to Washington*. The great Frank Capra directed both films. *It's a Wonderful Life* is a classic film that I watch every year. I had the privilege of narrating part of Mr. Capra's biography for audio. His son knew I was a big fan and asked me to be a part of the writing process. It was an honor. Frank Capra had a brilliant eye for capturing images and a great ability to write stories. He understood how to frame and block actors. The camera never got in the way of the story. Your attention was never on the camera but instead drawn into the story because of the way he used the camera.

Still, I think his biggest strength was his ability to work with actors, James Stewart in particular. Frank Capra knew how to get the best out of his actors in very challenging roles. Depicting the betrayal of a young man and his belief in our country's political system in *Mr. Smith Goes to Washington* was courageous at the time. He got a lot of criticism and U.S. Senator Joe McCarthy labeled him negatively and questioned his patriotism. Capra went through a great deal and is one of the best directors in my opinion. There were a lot of other people who also influenced me as a young director coming up in the industry and continue to impact me as a writer and producer: Melvin Van Peebles, Gordon Parks, Federico Fellini, Michael Schultz, Howard Thurman, George Lucas, and Steven Spielberg among them.

Melvin Van Peebles

Before Melvin Van Peebles became an artist, he was a successful stock-broker on Wall Street with the dream of becoming an artist. Peebles was a genius who wrote, produced, and directed *Sweet Sweetback's Baadasssss Song*. This was a film of courage because nobody had ever made a film like it. *Sweet Sweetback's Baadasssss Song* fit into the very fabric of the protest movement. It was about a defiant black man who fought back against his oppressors and won by escaping persecution. It was a shock to everybody but recognized as a pioneering effort. Melvin Van Peebles got our attention by producing, directing, writing, and starring in this film. Due to the subject matter, big studios wouldn't fund the film, so Peebles found the funding himself. The film was a great financial success and demonstrated the profitability of blaxploitation movies. This proved to studios the value of black audiences. Van Peebles did things his way and never watered down his truths. He showed you what you could do as a black artist.

Young people nowadays take working in the movie business for granted. There was a time when black directors, independent films, black actors, and black writers could not make a living with their craft. It's impossible to describe the importance of what creative pioneers like Gordon Parks and Melvin Van Peebles have done. Without their accomplishments, there would be no blacks in the movie industry because they laid the foundation for us to be seen and accepted.

Gordon Parks

Gordon Parks was a photographer turned filmmaker and the first African American filmmaker to produce and direct major motion pictures. He birthed the blaxploitation movement and directed the movie *Shaft*, the first of its kind. Gordon Parks created a black superhero who not only went up against the system, but also anybody in his neighborhood who did bad things. Shaft was black, courageous, kind, and dangerous all rolled into one. He dressed fly and wooed the women but also kicked the bad guys' butts. Gordon Parks created the foundation for many black hero films to come. He is responsible for laying the groundwork for many of the black male stars of today. Gordon was also a excellent still photographer with a great eye. If you look at his films carefully, you'll witness his artistry as a visionary.

A pinnacle moment in my life occurred on a PBS set for Lorraine Hansberry's film *A Raisin in the Sun* starring Danny Glover. As I was getting ready to go to lunch one day, my assistant tapped me on the shoulder and told me someone wanted to talk to me. When I turned around, my jaw dropped. I was in shock: there in front of me stood the great Gordon Parks. From the darkness of the stage, he had been observing my directing. He put out his hand

and said, "I'm Gordon Parks, young man. Keep on doing what you're doing. You're good at it." I was about to say thank you when he turned around and walked away. He looked back and smiled. It was an unforgettable moment. He didn't have to stop by the set and watch me work. He had no obligation to compliment me, but his generosity of heart encouraged me deeply. That encouragement came from a man whose work I deeply respected.

Federico Fellini

Federico Fellini was an Italian film director and screenwriter known as one of the most prominent filmmakers of all time. During his nearly fifty years in film, Fellini received twelve Academy Award nominations and four wins. Fellini had a unique style. His films are fantastical in nature and highlight the beauty in the ugliness of humanity.

Out of all the wonderful films that Federico Fellini directed, *8½* was my favorite because he did something unheard of at that time. He told the story in a non sequitur way. It was split among dream, fantasy, and reality but never lost the ability to make the audience care for the major characters. Fellini's ability to tell stories is unparalleled to this day. Sometimes people overcame their enemies. Sometimes the protagonist's enemies were self-inflicted wounds of confusion, doubt, or just being human. Fellini's ability to connect his audience to the humanity of his characters is what attracted me to his work. Seeing the nonlinear format of *8½* gave me the courage to rethink my approach to filmmaking.

Michael Schultz

Michael Schultz is also a great man. He gave me my first major directing job on a play called *Dream on Monkey Mountain*. Michael and I became friends when he was a primary director at the Negro Ensemble Company, which was then run by Robert Hooks and Douglas Turner Ward. Michael was supposed to direct *Dream on Monkey Mountain*, but he had a prior obligation to direct *Cooley High*. So he asked if I'd direct and I said yes. Michael went to direct one of the classics, *Cooley High*, starring Glynn Turman, Lawrence Hilton-Jacobs, and Garrett Morris.

Dream on Monkey Mountain was chosen to run in Berlin during the 1972 Summer Olympics in Germany. The play starred Roscoe Lee Brown and Ron O'Neal. Michael had already done a great deal of work on the play, so all I had to do was add some things and manage what he had already done. The play went on a couple times in Berlin, receiving standing ovations each time. Germans know how to drink, and they know how to party. The cast, crew, and I were invited to restaurants, clubs, and parties. They used to dance and drink. At that time, I was partially vegetarian but the days I spent in Germany, I don't think I saw one vegetable aside from a potato. They ate meat, meat, meat, and more meat. They ate beef, pork, chicken, lamb, deer, antelope, goat, oxtails, squirrels, rabbits, frog, alligator, sharks, and more. If you were hungry, you had one option: potatoes and meat. Then there was beer, beer, beer, and more beer. Dark beers. Light beers. Flavored beers. Bottled beers. Draught beers. It was beer heaven topped off by wines and champagnes. Most impressively, desserts were piled layers high on your plate. They would laugh and sing at the dinner table while staring at you until your plate was clean. We had a great time until I decided to be adventurous and rented a car to take a drive on the Autobahn.

I was driving 75 to 80 miles per hour, but cars were honking behind me because they thought I was going too slowly. Cars on my left and right were passing me at a minimum of 100 mph. Some restricted areas had speed limits, but other areas had no speed limits at all. I was told there were no accidents on the Autobahn, just deadly crashes. I got off as soon as I could, and it took me hours to get back to the hotel. I was glad I went because I had never had a driving experience like that in my life. When I returned to the states, I realized that we were wimps with speed limits of 30 to 65 miles per hour. A German lady laughed in my face when I told her that our speed limits were a maximum of 65 miles per hour. This experience would not have been possible without Michael Schultz. Years later, Michael asked me to audition for a role in his new film *Car Wash*. Michael Schultz, to a great extent, is responsible for my career as an actor and director.

Howard Thurman

Howard Thurman was a world-renowned philosopher, theologian, educator, author, and civil rights activist. He was greatly influenced by Mahatma Gandhi, whom he met during his Christian missionary work. During his encounter with Gandhi, Thurman was encouraged by Gandhi's message of peace. Thurman's theology, philosophy, and stance on nonviolence influenced major civil rights activists. Thurman was a mentor to

Dr. Martin Luther King Jr. and a classmate and friend of Dr. King's father when they attended Morehouse College. Thurman wrote more than twenty-one books about spiritual renewal. The Howard Thurman Center for Common Ground was established on his behalf at Boston University.

Thurman challenged all people to be personally responsible for their lives and the decisions that they make. Until I studied his words, I blamed my problems on others. *Our relationship failed because of her. I didn't get the job because America is racist. Life is unfair.* I never truly dug into the responsibility of my own choices, but after closer examination, I realized my experiences are based upon choices that I have made and to which I have given consent. I'm not suggesting that slavery does not continue to mark African Americans deeply in terms of emotional scars. I'm not suggesting racism and classism do not exist. I'm not suggesting that the impact of these things on our culture has not damaged us in many ways. But there is also a *so what?* factor. And the *so what?* factor is based upon Thurman's phrase "unless it has the mark of your inner authority."

There's an expectation in the minds of some that eventually things will be fine because someone is coming to save us. Suppose for a minute that it was proven that no one is coming. If no one is coming to save us, what options are we left with? We can sink into the mire of blame, we can march, we can protest, or as Malcom said, no matter how great a football player you are, if the name of the game is baseball, we can get ourselves a bat. Many of us are standing at home plate with a helmet on and a football in our hand. We are being the great football player we are, though the name of the game has changed and our competition is circling the bases in a game called baseball. We are not required to wake up, but if we do not, eventually the lights in the stadium will go dark, and nothing good awaits us in the darkness. Howard Thurman understood the game of life and politics. He also understood the game of the human spirit and taught me that once I took responsibility for my own life—successes and failures alike—no one could stop me from succeeding except me. I still believe that. Howard Thurman was lesser known than Dr. King but no less significant.

Sidney Poitier

In terms of my acting career, I had many great teachers who gave me courage, but no actor had a greater impact on my life and career than

Sidney Poitier. Many people criticized him for cooperating too much and were cynical about the characters he portrayed. I think these critics don't understand the time period in which Sidney grew up, and they undermine his pioneering. Sidney Poitier was in films during segregation, when the rules of the KKK were followed in many parts of the country. When he played Walter Lee in *A Raisin in the Sun*, it showed the dilemma and internal conflicts of black men in America. Walter did anything to help his family but was faced with the struggles of being a polite and submissive chauffeur for people who insulted him. He kept his dignity for his family. Sidney's role in *A Raisin in the Sun* changed my life. I could relate to that character and knew the soul of that character. Sidney went on to act in movies that showed black men standing up for themselves like *My Name Is Mr. Tibbs* and *Guess Who's Coming to Dinner*.

People today might not understand that this was unheard of back then. Sidney faced so much criticism, but it didn't stop him because he felt that he should have the same freedoms as white actors and that his career should not be limited in any way by his skin color. He did not allow color to be an issue. Sidney Poitier is one of the greatest and most courageous heroes of our time. He stood up for black people and had the courage not to limit himself to just acting, also pursuing producing, writing, and directing. Sidney and Harry Belafonte did things together that hadn't been done before; without them, there would be no black screen actors. They laid the groundwork so that people like me could succeed. One of the reasons I am writing this book is to solidify the importance of pioneering artists like Sidney Poitier, who paved the way for me do things I had only dreamed of doing.

I had the great fortune of having several conversations with Sidney Poitier, an insightful, brilliant, and humorous man who isn't afraid to state the truth. He is a walking encyclopedia of the history of Hollywood and what he went through. They wanted him to crawl on his knees in a film, and he refused, telling them he could say the same thing standing up. Sidney won that battle after much back-and-forth. He didn't do things like that only for himself but also for black people as a whole. Sidney went through so much behind the scenes; only those who know him were aware. We *do* know that he was criticized by white *and* black people for not being what they felt he was supposed to be. He was his own man and continued to make us proud.

Alex Haley

Alex Haley was another of the greatest thinkers and writers of our time. He died too young but his contribution to film, screenwriting, and this nation is something that will live forever. He created the television miniseries *Roots*. Nobody expected *Roots* to be a success. I was told the networks were terrified of a show that depicted all black people during slavery showing what America had done to them. It depicted white people taking black people from Africa to the auction block in America and from there to plantations. *Roots* was a groundbreaking venture for America because black people learned something about themselves. White people learned something about the history of this nation, how blacks were treated, and African culture.

I remember the scene when the slave masters tried to make the young slave change his name from Kunta Kinte to Toby. I vividly remember the beating that it took to get Kunta to submit. It was hard to watch. He symbolically expressed what all Africans went through in terms of the submission to Western civilizations. Our gods, our religion, our culture, our rituals, and our history were destroyed. We were told to adjust and assimilate. We were animals taken from our shores on a gruesome journey west, yet we survived. We made it through some of the most horrific and genocidal experiences ever faced by mankind. Alex Haley had the courage to show where we came from, where we've been, and what we've become.

Historically speaking, *Roots* is one of the most viewed television shows in the history of this nation. It wasn't watched only by blacks but by people of all backgrounds. *Roots* showed people a different perspective. Alex Haley established his greatness with that series, but later he and the great Norman Lear, the most prolific producer at that time, teamed up to create a show called *Palmerstown, U.S.A.*

I costarred in that series with Michael J. Fox and Jonelle Allen. *Palmerstown* was a life-changing experience for me because I wasn't a bad guy like in many of the films I had done to that point. I was chosen to play Luther Freeman, the father of a nuclear family who lived near a white family in the South during segregation. Luther's son and the white man's son became friends. The show examined their friendship and how it impacted the behavior, feelings, and thoughts of the adults. The writing was excellent.

The show realistically depicted the damaging effects of racism as the two families grew closer. *Palmerstown* posed challenging questions about prejudice: Does it occur because we are black and prejudged by white America, or because we are white and prejudged by black America, or are we simply human beings who should embrace our commonalities and celebrate our differences? Alex Haley and Norman Lear celebrated our differences as black and white cultures but consistently pointed to the commonalities of our humanity. Both families in the show had marital, parenting, and financial problems, things families can identify with regardless of color. It was humanity far before color. To this day, I praise Norman Lear and Alex Haley for their great insight. The show lasted two seasons. I loved working on this show and thought it was an important vision that taught a great deal to America.

Miles Davis

Music has been influential in my life as well. In the '80s, I went to a concert at the Lincoln Center, and I sat down with my then girlfriend. Miles Davis, in my opinion the greatest trumpet player and musician who ever lived, sat down in front of me.

He turned around and said, "You Bill Duke?"

I said, "Yes sir."

"I like your acting," he continued.

I replied, "Mr. Davis, your music is something I cannot express."

He whispered, "Thank you. Thank you."

It felt amazing and overwhelming being in the presence of Miles Davis. I cannot fully express my gratitude to him for creating romantic and soothing music to temper my moments of rage as a young man. I didn't listen to jazz very much before Mile Davis. It was too complex and complicated for me with too many notes. When he slowed things down and sped them up again and played with John Coltrane and Dizzy Gillespie, I understood better. I understood Herbie Hancock. I understood John Coltrane. I understood all of the greats like Louis Armstrong. I understood the depths of their pain. Charlie Mingus. Thelonious Monk. I understood the off notes of Monk. I understood the depth of Mingus's bass. I understood not on an intellectual level, but in the depths of my soul. I understood not as a black man, but as a human being that through music you can be healed, helped, and understood. You can relate, have dialogue and feelings, and have a sense of who you were without a spoken word.

The truth is, as I sat behind Miles Davis, I wanted to hug him and kiss the back of his head and tell him about the many nights he had created romance and the nights that he had enabled me to heal from the pain that I was going through. Miles Davis was my inspiration. He was a spirit who gave me comfort. I don't think I heard the rest of the concert that night. I don't even remember who was onstage. I just sat there in appreciation and awe of Miles Davis.

Dick Gregory

I was in awe of another man for many different reasons. Mr. Dick Gregory was a friend of mine whom I had known for many years. I was in speechless pain when he passed away. It made me reflect on my own life. I want to be able to leave behind something of value. What I can leave does not compare to what those who have come before me have left. Dick's death was the end of an era. It was the death of a generation of heroes who believed their lives were secondary to the cause of their people. Dick Gregory reminded me so much of other great ones in our community who have passed on, like Medgar Evers, Dr. King, Malcolm X, Rosa Parks, Stokely Carmichael, James Baldwin, Sojourner Truth, and many more who made it their life mission to free black people from a slave consciousness. They believed something larger than their own lives chose them to free their people. They were willing to die for the cause and many of them did. They, along with many others, nameless and in large numbers, stood up and told the truth. Because our people have been lied to by so many, telling the truth made them leaders. Their truths also gave hope that something better could happen.

I feel as though they have asked us for something. They have asked us to love ourselves as much as they did, act out of love for ourselves and each other, make the sacrifices necessary for survival and self-regard in the deepest sense of the word. The legacy we leave our children is based upon what we do today and not what we plan to do tomorrow. We cannot punish ourselves for what we have done or have not done, because humanity is always full of successes and defeats. We must continue to understand that we have an obligation, a responsibility, a duty to the next generation of children, no matter what color they may be. We have the duty to give them something that enables them to make a better life for themselves than we had. We are surrounded by a world of suffering with wars, famine, poverty, and begging.

The world is full of people escaping to different countries in order to save their children and others. The suffering is one thing but what gives you hope are the brave souls who stood up and spoke of that suffering and were willing to put their lives on the line to stop that suffering. Dick Gregory was one of those human beings. He spoke truth from his soul, not just to get attention, but also to spread information that he felt was valuable to the salvation of the world. He didn't speak truth only to white people or the system, he also spoke to black people. He talked about our cowardice and our ignorance. He shined light on the fact that we wouldn't take up for our own.

Dick Gregory would go to churches and demand that they take down "that white-faced Jesus" because Jesus looked like *us*. Dick Gregory was the first black comedian to perform at the Playboy Club and the first black comedian to be a guest on *The Tonight Show*. After overcoming some health issues, he became a nutritional activist who advocated for a raw food diet. He was the reason I became a vegetarian for many years, and I still eat a vegan diet several days a week. You feel better when you don't consume the carnage of dead flesh. My whole family eats meat. I love chicken and fish, but it's a lifestyle choice.

Dick Gregory and many like him didn't just talk about politics, they put their lives on the line. Dick Gregory implied in his last years that as a race and a culture, we are cowards. We don't stand up anymore. He talked about the gathering of mental, physical, economic, and spiritual resources in our community. We once had banks and black Wall Street during segregation, but during integration we moved away from working with each other. Dick said we have become buffoons and clowns to the rest of the world because we refuse to stand up. He'd say we deserve to be laughed at because we are cowards. I went through a lot of self-examination due to Dick Gregory. I think the men of my generation are cowards because we haven't devoted ourselves to something more important than our survival, and as a result our children are doing the same. The marches are okay, but why aren't we marching in our own communities to better our own conditions when we have the intellect and ability to do so? Most minorities, especially black people, are alchemists and we've proven our alchemy.

Jesus was the first alchemist, turning water into wine, but black people were thrown the hooves of pigs, so we seasoned them and made pigs feet. We were given the guts of the pig and washed them and turn them into chitlins. We are alchemists and what we have done today is given up on our alchemy. The great music of our time comes out of our alchemy. Jazz, blues, and rap are products of our alchemy. The ability to turn pain into art is the result of alchemy. It takes courage to speak truth through art, but very few of us stand up anymore. We have become comfortable and complacent.

Our boys are being murdered in the streets, and we blame the system. To a certain extent, that is true. I do not condone police officers killing young unarmed boys for any reason and being acquitted of those actions, but there are so many other layers to it. Kids graduate with second-grade reading skills and have babies at the age of fourteen or fifteen. Grandmas are in their early thirties. I know it has to do with the system and overwhelming poverty, but when the giant has his foot on your neck, you have a couple of options. You can let him keep pushing until he snaps your neck or you can bite his toe. We have to utilize all that enables us to resist the madness of oppression.

We are constantly waiting on someone to save us, but nobody is coming. We should be saving ourselves. I am not appalled by the fact that we blame the system and police for the deaths of young men, but the honest truth is that we are killing more of each other than the police ever have. The record numbers of slaughters of each other has given permission and approval for others to do the same. We are saying we aren't worthy and have no value. We base our worth on someone else's actions: you are coming on my turf, you didn't deliver the drugs, you're a Crip or a Blood, you are lighter or darker, or you stepped on my shoes. It is savage ignorance. Everybody wants to know what would happen if Dr. King came back today. I think Dr. King is watching and saying, "I ain't comin' back." I think Malcolm and Medgar are saying, "I ain't comin' back." They are looking at us as crazy and cowardly. When I hear the rationale behind some of our behavior, I think *really*? Young girls are being molested by family members and excuses are made to justify these actions? They are doing it because they don't know any better or because someone did it to them when they were younger. The excuses continue.

People ask me when it will stop and I have no idea, but I do know that unless we stop, we are passing things down to our children that no responsible human being should ever hand to a child: we are passing down the weight and burden of irresponsibility. We are cowards because we no longer trust each other or ourselves. We are afraid to collaborate because of the possible consequences. We are the consequences of our cowardice. I'm not talking about rebellion; I'm talking about simple dignity, respect for women, and collaboration.

Brave men like Dick Gregory gave life to this way of thinking and held us accountable. He understood that the foundation of our survival depends upon collectivism. Aside from church, sororities, fraternities, and historically black colleges, there is no gathering of black people coming together to find solutions to problems that we mutually face. I am hoping and praying that someday it will happen. I pray that within us the spirit of grace and courage reunites itself and relights itself so we can be the beacon of the future for our children. Without that light, we will continue to live in darkness.

When I saw Dick Gregory perform, he was more than a black comedian. He was a universal voice of truth, and he spoke to blacks, whites, Asians, Latinos. He spoke to us all from his spirit. He tried to protect us from what he felt was dangerous to us. He sacrificed family and fortune. He sacrificed so much for truth because his spirit lived deeply, nourished with the truth. He could have become much wealthier if he had kept his mouth shut. He could have been more famous if he had made his message more subtle, but he chose not to because it would have compromised his soul. It would have compromised his spirit, and the compromise of the human spirit always leads to something worse.

The day he died was tragic for me, but he left us something. He left us an example to follow in terms of what is possible. During the wonderful pioneering moments of his life, it was my honor to know him and speak with him often. We loved and respected each other. When I gained his respect, it was a big moment for me, because he always wanted you to know where you stood in his reality. If you were not contributing to something larger than your ego, he called you on it. I loved Dick Gregory because he helped me love myself. He let our country love itself more by recognizing the truth that he courageously and fearlessly exposed.

BEE BOP

Outside's fine
And I guess that's the way it's supposed to be
Outside's fine
But that's got nothin' to do with me
Outside things are going swell
But I'm at the bottom of a wishin' well
Cold as hell
Inside
Outside things are goin' fine: smellin' flowers
Drinkin' wine
Lovin' people
Bein' kind
Refined
But inside things are ready to bust
Mistrust is turnin' my love to lust
Confusion's makin' fun of hate
All my earlies come too late
Identity treats me like a dog
And all of it's driftin' through a fog
Inside
Outside's goin' around givin' advice
Tellin' folks that bad is nice
And how great things must have been for Christ
Because he was willin' to pay the price
But inside
The price has never been paid
And all except delusions fade
Like limping shadows across a shade
Of all my broken promises made
Afraid
Outside's fine
And I guess that's the way it's supposed to be
Outside's fine

But that's got nothin' to do with me
Outside things are goin' swell
But I'm at the bottom of a wishin' well
Cold as hell
Inside

Chapter 11

A POOL OF REGRET

On the tree of life, some fruit hangs no lower than our self-perception.
—Bill Duke

LIFE IN NEW YORK CITY IN the 1970s was always a struggle. Each day, I rode the bus on my way uptown, passing the usual assortment of slums and junkies as I traveled northward past construction projects, stores, and produce vendors. There were men on street corners gesturing and talking to themselves and women and children moving in slow motion. The bus driver's head was bigger than his hat. His face was not black and not white but gray with the repetitious announcement of the stops. As I rode north, Bob Dylan, the Beatles, the Rolling Stones, John Coltrane, Miles Davis, the Drifters, Aretha Franklin, Marvin Gaye, the Temptations, Mozart, Puccini, Paul Robeson, and more played a symphony in what used to be my brain.

Getting high was my lowest point. I had no center that I could remember. I forgot what Mama, Daddy, Uncle Albert, Grandma, Grandpa, family, and friends had told me about the world. A world of racism. A world of rejection. Lectures about resilience. Sermons about God and Jesus. The trials and tribulations of Christian beliefs. The salvation of Jesus, Buddha, and Muhammed. All the tools of survival they'd given me collapsed into a pool of regret. Regret that I had not taken the advice of all of those who doubted me and told me that I was too tall, too dark, too ugly, and too untalented to become anything other than a grocery bagger at the A&P. I felt the rejection of all I auditioned for, of all my dreams by those who could have fulfilled them. The sad faces of my parents and family, who looked upon me with pity, compassion, and regret. I remember the many nights of ramen noodle soup dinners. The days of stealing from stores and hearts and trust. The hours of looking into mirrors and seeing a shadow of what once existed.

THE RAINCOAT

I lived on 2nd Street, and my lady and I hadn't eaten for a couple of days because my unemployment had run out. Against the wishes of my girlfriend, I decided to take my chances at theft. I went to the closet, grabbed my raincoat, and sewed pieces of a cut-up sheet to the inside, creating three gigantic pockets. These pockets would hold—and hide—anything I decided to take from the local supermarket. The pockets were large enough to hold small packages of meat, cookies, and anything else that was flat enough to not create bulges.

With my girlfriend as the lookout, we made a plan. As a distraction, she shopped with the last $10 we had for beans and soup while I went down other aisles, picking up as much as I could conceal in my new pockets. I spotted a security guard at the end of one aisle. He was a *brotha*. He looked at me. I smiled, but he didn't smile back. I wasn't bothered because I had already finished filling my new pockets by the time I saw him. I met my girlfriend at the checkout counter, where she was in a panic as she waited to pay for cans of food. She said I should put everything back as soon as possible because the security guard had been watching us the entire time. She thought he saw me take meat from the deli section.

I thought that was impossible because I had looked around before sliding it into my raincoat. She began to cry and insist that I put everything back. I turned away from her and carefully returned everything that I had stolen. She put the soup cans on the counter and prepared to pay. The security guard approached me along with the store manager, taking me to the side. The security guard scowled at me with disgust as the manager—a short, balding white man with red hair and a graying mustache—said gently, "Sir, would you mind opening your coat?" I asked him why, and he said, "Sir, please, I'm asking you to open your raincoat so I may see the inside." I feigned indignation.

"Is there a problem here?" I asked.

The manager responded, "Sir, if you do not open your raincoat, we will be forced to call the police." I looked at them. They looked at me. My girlfriend stood frozen. I opened my jacket. They saw the sewn pockets, but they were empty.

The security guard turned to the owner, "You see? I told you." Then he turned to me. "You stole the meat, the food, and the candy. I followed you and I saw you put them in your pockets."

Slowly, I turned each pocket inside out. "What candy? What meat? What food? What are you talking about?"

The manager asked why I had pockets sewn inside my raincoat. I told him that I was taking classes in fashion design and I was working on a new concept, adding, "It's really none of your damn business." The manager and the security guard exchanged dismayed looks. "Is this a racial issue?" I asked. The manager wanted to know what I meant by that. I then said with forced indignation, "It's raining outside and there are white men in this store with rain coats on. Why am I the only man being stopped? Because I'm black? You should be ashamed of yourselves." With that, my girlfriend grabbed the groceries we had paid for and left the store.

As we crossed the street on our way to my apartment building, nothing was said aloud but much was said in our silence. We laughed about the insanity of it all, but thankfully we made those beans and soups last by eating small portions with pieces of bread for about ten days. After eating very little and consuming the last of the drugs I had, I sat in in the bathroom and stared in the mirror at someone I used to be. Every day I looked for work, but I was turned down at every audition. I stopped taking acting classes. I washed every day, but my clothes smelled of the stench of desperation. I was desperate and destitute.

DO YOUR MAMA KNOW?

One day after panhandling in front of my building for rent money, I stood there among a void of passing strangers whom I hated for being able to wear suits, hats, dresses, shined shoes, and attitudes of confidence and success—and for passing me by with eyes of condemnation, disgust, and snickering judgment. With a mixture of humility and anger, I held out my hand to receive whatever scrap anyone would give me. It was not only a low time, but a time of crisis for me. Not a career crisis, a life crisis, a crisis of questions with no answers. A crisis of *They were right. I should've listened. I'm a failure. I have no talent. How stupid. How irresponsible.* A time of lying alone in the dark, not asleep but not fully awake. A time of wiping the dust off the shoes that had no possibility of ever being shined again.

An elderly black woman in her late eighties approached me one day while I was begging for change. "Ma'am, could you spare some change?" I asked the question and her eyes never left my eyes, but she walked past me with no comment. I asked the next two people the same question before felt a finger tapping my shoulder. I turned to see the old lady who had passed me earlier. I thought maybe she'd had a change of heart. She looked in my eyes as I asked again. "Ma'am, can you spare any change?" She was silent for a moment, continuing to meet my gaze. After what seemed like forever, I began getting annoyed, so I broke the silence. "Ma'am, can you hear me? Can you spare some change?"

After a beat or two, she replied, "Baby, do your mama know you out here doin' this?" I wasn't sure I heard her right, so I asked her to repeat herself. "I said," she replied, "do your mama know you out here doin' this?"

I looked at her in stunned silence, a timeless moment of awareness, and she looked at me, too. She smiled, shook her head, and walked away. I watched her slowly cross the next block until she disappeared from sight. I turned, sat down on the front steps of my building, and bowed my head in my hands. I kept my eyes and my mind open. After maybe an hour or two, I slowly climbed four stories' worth of steps to my apartment. I read the eviction notice on my door, turned the knob, and then sat in silence and darkness, simmering in the pain I was in.

Something deep within me changed that day. Even though I knew that within ten days I'd be forced to leave that apartment and that I had no money and no prospects for work, I knew for sure that I would never beg anyone for change again. It was just such a challenging time, not only for me, but for everyone I knew. And, I suppose, as a way to cope, everyone I knew partied. I didn't know anyone who *didn't* take drugs. It was every-where, like air.

I was at a party and a friend of mine had heroin on his pinky and put it in front of my nose. I was so high on other drugs that I was about to snort it before my friend John stopped me. Weed was recreational and didn't seem addictive, but I was hooked on hashish and cocaine and I eventually tried LSD. I guess this was my way of escaping the pressures of the industry I'd chosen. I already had self-esteem issues and the constant rejection just added to that. I'd go on countless auditions—at least twelve and sometimes up to fifteen a week—without a callback. It created so much doubt and pain inside me. I guess I was trying to relieve that oppressive frustration with drugs and partying.

The first time I took LSD was at a party. When I got back to my apartment, I was so paranoid that I thought aliens were coming after me, so I got naked and hopped in the bathtub. I heard the door open. I was ready to throw a spear at my sister and her husband because I thought they were aliens. They calmed me down, put water in the bathtub, eased the paranoia out of me, and brought me back to reality.

JW SMITH

I finally moved uptown to 91st Street with my good friend, JW, and as usual we were poor as hell. We were good friends from acting classes who didn't have much money, but somehow we managed. It was hand to mouth most days. We used to put our change together and pray that we'd have enough to buy some food. We did whatever we could to survive. Sometimes, JW would stay with me, and sometimes he lived elsewhere and I'd find other roommates. It depended on the circumstances. When I didn't have money to pay my share of the rent, which was about once every four months, he would help me find a temporary place that I could move into. We'd scrounge up a couple of rusty old shopping carts to put my file cabinets, luggage, and whatever else I had in, then we'd roll them to my next pad. Those shopping carts were a permanent part of my reality and a visual reminder of how little I owned. It was both a blessing and a jolt of reality to realize that I could transport all of my possessions in those rickety old metal carts with wobbly wheels.

One time, JW and I took a class in theater management and for once we had enough money to get the subway downtown but not enough to get back. I lived downtown, and the class was on the other side of the city.

We had two options: either we could take the subway back uptown and not eat, or we could eat and walk the almost ninety blocks back. We were both hungry, so we decided to eat at a restaurant in the Village. And then we walked and walked and walked. We walked all the way from the Village to 91st Street. We walked for hours that day. Between walking, sharing a closet with a cat, and begging for money, my dream of acting was a real challenge. I never regretted my decision to become an actor, and I never said I couldn't do it. I was willing to endure whatever I had to in order to do what I felt was my calling.

It was not easy, but I am glad I did—and continue to do it. Those hard times of walking long distances and skipping meals were worth it, but back then, I wasn't always sure I'd make it out alive.

Chapter 12

MEDITATION

We learn wisdom from failure much more than from success.
—Samuel Smiles

MEDITATION DID NOT COME EASILY TO me. After Gilbert Moses got me my acting job in *Ain't Supposed to Die a Natural Death*, I continued to take drugs, and by then it was a habit I depended upon daily. The drugs made me irresponsible in terms of basic life choices. I neglected friends, family, and my own self-regard. I had been late to the play several times. Finally, the stage manager told me if I was late again, I would not be going onstage. The next time I arrived late, my understudy went on stage for me while I was forced to watch from the balcony. After observing Ted Lange (from *That's My Mama* and *The Love Boat*) perform my role, I realized that I could soon lose my job.

My friend Aida saw my condition and said that she saw me sliding downhill, soon to hit rock bottom. She knew I needed help and offered to teach me transcendental meditation. First, I thought it was a very hippie statement. I had no idea what meditation was. I thought it was hippies closing their eyes and humming in beds before having orgiastic sex. She explained to me that meditation reduces stress and provides focus and clarity of mind if done consistently. She didn't know what my pain was about but knew that if I continued down the road I was on, I would not survive. I loved her as a friend, but I thought she sounded a little wacky, so I blew her off.

There was no denying that I was a drughead in New York City. A few weeks later, I tripped on acid and a few days after that I had a series of hallucinations. One occurred when I was moving from my downtown apartment to a new apartment. I had paint cans and brushes and intended on painting the walls and ceiling of the new place. While on the bus, I saw people looking at me and I got paranoid. A lady with a sunken face and hair growing from her chin stared directly at me with one eye, the other closed. In another seat, a couple with matching clothes and red-and-black plaid hats moved their heads in an attempt to get my attention, and a pregnant woman accused me of something I didn't do. I looked out the window to my right and saw a dark cloud that was quickly moving toward me. I reached my bus stop, got off the bus, crossed the street, and walked down the sidewalk toward my apartment. I knew that cloud was following me and that the FBI and CIA had sent the secret cloud filled with poison gas to kill me. The cloud kept up with me. I walked as fast as I could to my block. The faster I walked, the closer the cloud got. As the cloud got closer to my head, I bent lower until I was crawling on the sidewalk with two paint cans and several brushes in my hands. I saw shoes, red-and-black sandals, bare feet, blisters, and boots, as I crawled by.

I saw spiders get stepped on, dust, vomit, and spit. I saw water from hoses cleaning the stench from the previous night, week, and year. There were eyes of rage and stares of confusion, eyes of pity, fear, condemnation, and laughter. There were old eyes and sunglassed eyes looking down at me. When I crawled up the stairs to my apartment, I crawled through the door and locked it behind me so the cloud couldn't get in. I scraped the walls of their paint and plaster until there was a large pile in the middle of the floor and then I fell into the pile and passed out. When I woke up with paint chips and garbage stuck to my face and body, I realized I had to do something. The next time Aida called me about meditation, I told her yes.

She came to my apartment and taught me transcendental meditation, but I continued to take drugs. After two or three weeks, she checked back with me and noticed not much had changed, so she made me an offer. She said she wanted to make a deal: She wanted me to meditate for the next three weeks without taking drugs of any kind, and if at the end of those three weeks I still wanted to do drugs, she'd buy me an ounce of anything I wanted. I was excited about this offer—in three weeks I would have an ounce of the drug of my choice! What more could an addict ask for?

That Monday I started my meditation and gave up drugs and alcohol. The first three days, I felt relaxed but still hungered for that high. At the beginning of the second week, something happened to me that I still don't fully understand. All I can say is that I felt more grounded, more centered, and without a sense of desperate need for alcohol and drugs to kill the pain. Much of the emotional pain I had felt prior to meditation was neutralized. By the end of the third week, I found my center, my core, my vortex, and with it came a sense of calmness. The emotional pain that drugs and alcohol used to numb was dissolved by my meditation techniques.

Aida saved my life. She believed in me, and she gave me hope. Through transcendental meditation I have been able to achieve a great deal; it has given me hope and confidence I did not have before. Most importantly, though, it put me in touch with a creative power I never knew existed. It flows through all of us if we have the tools to perceive and use it. I've meditated every day since the '70s, and it has truly changed my life. Guru Dev and Maharishi Mahesh Yogi brought transcendental meditation to the Western world. Their wisdom, insight, and compassion have saved many lives and souls—including mine.

MEN LIKE ME (PART 3)

Men like me
Carry signs on corners begging
For change to come
Or dress in suits that never fit
In the eyes of those who wonder
This fool must really think we're dumb
Where's that nigger really comin' from
And we feel it
But zip our lips with nothing to say
Cause we have mountains and mountains of bills to pay
Filled with hate that you take out on you
And everything that loves you too
Like my my my what am I gonna do
Yo my man am I getting thru
Men like me

Part IV

<hr>

MY CAREER

On the set of *Sister Act 2. From the author's collection*

Chapter 13

ACTING OUT

Aspire to inspire before you expire.—Unknown

WHAT IS REHEARSAL? REHEARSAL IS A practice of acting out, thinking, and speaking your words in a scene over and over and over and over again. First, you rehearse alone and in private. Then, you go over it (and over and over and over again) with the other actors. If you're lucky enough, then you are left alone with no script. At this point, it's just you, the scene, and other actors. Even though the blocking of the scene might be the same, what you rehearsed and what you do on the set is not. The rehearsal is preparing you to let go of the lines and the insecurities of surrendering to the moment.

You don't want to rehearse the exact way you're going to say your lines or the way you're going to do the scene. You are rehearsing to memorize the lines and let them live within you as a character. At the beginning of my acting career, when I went onstage, what I rehearsed is what I did. Because I felt safe, I said and did exactly what I rehearsed. I always knew something was missing and I could never describe what it was. I observed the great actors, and they really don't know how they're going to do something. They know the context. They respond to what the other person said because they are listening, not thinking. A lot depends on what the other people in the scene do. It's a matter of trust.

You have to trust your own instincts. I know there are many people who disagree with me, but I don't believe acting is doing what you rehearsed. The rehearsal prepares you to do and be in the moment in front of the camera or on stage in front of an audience. There is something that comes alive when you trust. If you don't trust it, your best performance is buried within you. The minute you let go of the lines, that's when the true story and the true character emerge. There's a freedom that comes from trusting yourself. You feel free of restraint and containment. You feel free of self-critique, one of the biggest challenges to overcome.

Sometimes we watch ourselves do it and we want to be better, so we plan out how we're going to say it and how are going to do it and how we're going to hold our hands or our shoulders. I am not putting down anyone who does that, but there is something more to be added. God has given you a gift of *being*. You're not sure how it's going to turn out every time but if you're there, the director will make the adjustments, not you. Self-adjustment. It's called stage fright because you're watching yourself as you're doing it. It is an incredible and sacred experience when you trust yourself enough to let go of your ego and intellect so that the spirit of your creativity comes out.

THE BUSINESS

The *business* of acting is a multilayered, fascinating, and necessary reality for actors today because most people come into the industry with passion for and an understanding of acting opportunities. They have in mind what movies they want to be in and what actors they want to be like. They want fame and fortune, longevity, and recognition. There are all kinds of reasons people come into this industry. It's sad when they have no understanding of the business aspect; they are crushed after working for five years as a server in a restaurant. You see people trying to survive rather than realizing their dreams. I've worked in restaurants, cleaned floors, and panhandled on street corners, but I wish I had known then just how much of a business this industry is and what kinds of sacrifices one has to make to survive. I wish someone had told me that when I was coming up, and I wish somebody had told me that it doesn't last forever.

This industry is like a roller coaster. It's up and it's down, it's down and it's up, it's left and it's right, it's over and it's under. The older actors move on for whatever reason, and the younger generation moves in, hoping to duplicate the successes they have seen. You have to be smart with the money you make and prepare in advance, so that you don't go broke when the roller coaster goes down—and it will go down. Are you spending all your money on materialistic things that you never had before? Can you actually afford the car, the house, the vacations, and the clubs with bottle service? After a certain amount of money, we can afford to do some of that, but even then, people still go broke because they don't listen to financial advisers. Money in this industry is the power to survive. When things are going great, you don't have to worry about basics like food, clothing, and shelter. It's about more than just saving, it's about using it to your advantage. What is money? How do you prepare for those moments, days, weeks, months, or even years when you're not working? You never know when—or if—the next job will roll around. What do you do in the meantime? Whose advice do you take? How do you understand the business side?

Most people focus on the "show" but neglect the "business." It's either something they don't want to face or something they just don't care about. It's important to prepare for those income droughts, and the best way to do that is to hire someone who knows more about money than you do—a business manager, financial adviser, or an accountant—who you can trust to track how you use your money. From there, keep an eye on the direction the industry is moving, because it shifts with each generation and technological advancement. You have to be prepared to shift with it.

Strategic alliances are just as important as money, sometimes maybe more so. There are people who know how to do certain things better than you, and those people are a great asset to your circle. For instance, you may be a great actor but not a great writer or director. If you create strategic alliances with folks who are good at those things, there's an opportunity to collaborate. With this collaboration, you create your own content. *It's Always Sunny in Philadelphia* started as webisodes until Danny DeVito caught wind of it and helped to turn it into one of the longest running live-action sitcoms in American TV history. Another example is *Awkward Black Girl* by Issa Rae, which started as a web series but became an HBO series called *Insecure*.

The film industry is now the media industry. When I was growing up there was no Internet or social media. There was no Hulu, Netflix, Amazon, Crackle, Verizon, and all the other content outlets. The opportunities that exist within these platforms are endless. It's important to understand your passion, but passion without an understanding of the industry leads to frustration and dismay. Today, more opportunities exist for talent than ever before because of the technology available. In the past, success was based on someone discovering your abilities. There are hundreds of people who come to Los Angeles every day by bus, train, and plane. They have hope that someone in that town will recognize their talent and give them the opportunity to be successful.

There's nothing wrong with that, it's just that today, you can "discover yourself." There are numerous examples of people who got tired of waiting to be discovered. They created their own webisodes, and once they developed their audience, it attracted sponsors and sometimes networks. Having a large and loyal audience has great value. In this instance, you discover yourself through your own efforts and ingenuity. Once you have discovered yourself and have let your discovery manifest itself into a global platform, people start looking at you differently. You're not someone begging for a shot, you created your *own* shot, and now *they* want to be part of that. Those are the fundamental ways to survive the industry, not only as a talent, but as a business-minded person.

Another good piece of advice is to always think in terms of franchise. One intellectual piece of property can generate multiple income streams. Take Disney, the master of all franchises, as an example. Disney will take an idea such as a comic book, novel, film, or animation, and give it its own movie and brand. Along with the brand comes merchandise, and along with the merchandise comes a theme park ride. In the end, one piece of intellectual property has been franchised into multiple income streams. Wouldn't it be nice if you had one idea—a book, television series, or animation—that blossomed into mugs, T-shirts, hats, and dolls? You own it all: the trademark, copyright, and the license to the concept. This is about the future. I advise you all to watch an online video called *Humans Need Not Apply*. It is frighteningly insightful.

CAR WASH

My first big break came by referral. The making of the movie *Car Wash* was a pinnacle moment for me because I had done smaller films but never a major motion picture. My friend Michael Schultz had come to Hollywood a couple of years before me and when I came to town with Lloyd Richards, I was told there was an audition for *Car Wash*, so I went. Michael Schultz thought I was right for the part and hired me. The cast featured great comedians and actors from Antonio Fargas to James Spinks, Henry Kingi, George Carlin, Danny DeVito, Richard Pryor, the Pointer Sisters, and on and on. The way that Michael used the music for the movie and the way he put everything together was incredible and groundbreaking.

The script had a real message in terms of what young black men were going through at that time, which my character, Raheem, symbolized. Raheem showed the rage and anger that young black men felt toward the system. We were in a situation of desperation because no one could "hear" our voices. The anger in my character and the anger in Ivan Dixon's character, Lonnie, manifested itself in different ways. The characters had been through similar challenges, but Lonnie dealt with his rage through peaceful means and became the best at his job. He was Raheem's best friend at the car wash and Raheem respected and loved him.

At a point when he just couldn't take any more from the boss and his son, my character decided to quit the car wash. In an effort to get even, he returned to rob the place. Raheem was desperate for money and angry because the car wash represented the white man getting over on him. He was also mad at the Uncle Toms of the world.

Richard Pryor played a preacher who rode around in his nice car and pimped out women. Raheem soon found out from the Pointer Sisters that speaking out wasn't the best idea, but at least he expressed how he was feeling. Richard Pryor as an actor was one thing, but on the set as a person he came in with such humility and respect. He was at the top of his game then, and we expected a major star to walk in with a bit of an ego, but that was not the case. He almost hid in the corners. When he was on the set, he gave 1,000 percent and when he wasn't on the set he returned to his car. The lines were written, but it made no difference because Richard said whatever he wanted to say and did whatever he wanted to do. Michael understood that and let him do it because whatever Richard came up with was always better than what had been written. It was wonderful, and we did not know what to expect as actors because the Pointer Sisters were always singing a song while he was speaking. There was so much going on.

The audience's reaction at the premiere was powerful. The most moving scene was when my character went to rob the car wash and Ivan Dixon's character told me not to and I break down in his arms. This scene was also painful because I wasn't acting. I was a young man frustrated with Hollywood and all its politics. I was fascinated with all the difficulties a black man faced coming up in the entertainment business. It was easy for me to feel Raheem's rejection, submission, and anger, because it was something I was going through at the time. So many black men in America identified with that, and some of them thanked me afterward, adding that my role reflected feelings that we have and aren't often able to express. I was so happy and proud to be a part of the movie and of Michael Schultz's vision. I enjoyed watching Danny DeVito and George Carlin, who was a genius. It was a star-packed cast and also a friend-packed movie. We loved each other on that set. We went on a national tour with the movie. There are certain cities we probably could never go back to because of our epic celebrations but we ate and drank and had a good time. I am so glad I was a part of *Car Wash* and that *Car Wash* was, and is, a part of me.

AMERICAN GIGOLO

American Gigolo came next, and it was a challenge for me in many ways. It was a great role and working with the talented Richard Gere was spectacular. He always came prepared, which challenged me to be just as prepared because if I wasn't, he'd blow me away on screen. When I say prepare, I don't just mean practice: he *lives* in the moment of the character. One of the most powerful traits of Richard Gere as an actor is that he listens and responds to costars based upon what they do and say. The challenging part of my role was that my character, Leon, was bisexual. I was really worried about this because as a black man in Hollywood, I felt like I represented black people as a whole, whether I wanted to or not. I was nervous about how my parents, family, and black people in general would judge me for playing a black bisexual pimp. I struggled with it, but after talking to my agent and manager at the time, I decided my career was more important to me than what others thought of me or even what I thought of myself.

That particular role was powerful. It was one of those roles where I had to dig deep. Leon was nice on the surface but a deceptive human being. He was charming, smiled widely, and knew how to deal with those who worked for him. He was also a narcissist and a sadist who liked to torture people under his power. I had to find his humanity, which was in his paranoia that everyone was after him. He didn't trust anybody, and because of this, he had to control everything and everyone under him. He couldn't reveal that, so he dressed elegantly no matter where he was. Leon was a fascinating character. The way he talked was also important. He wasn't a fast talker but a very calculated one. Everything about him was calculated, down to how he moved his hand or his finger. Richard Gere was meticulous with every movement of his character, like the movement of the eyes, the face, the lips, the hands, and the legs. It was a great experience. I found it to be one of the high points of my acting career with one of the leading roles of the film. It was outside of my comfort zone, but it was a growing experience. I loved the character I played, and I loved working with Richard Gere.

The subject matter of the film didn't bother me, although a movie about a gigolo was definitely controversial at that time. It was a great script written and directed by Paul Schrader. Working with Paul was an honor. He was one of my favorite writers and directors at that time. He had written and directed *Blue Collar*, which starred Richard Pryor and Yaphet Kotto. It was a film that helped shape my directing career and impacted my writing. Anyone who hasn't seen *Blue Collar* should watch it.

Having the opportunity to work with a hero of mine was a real privilege. On set Paul was always prepared with a vision of how each scene should be blocked and where the camera should be placed long before the actors arrived. As an actor if you had an idea about your character or if, for example, you wanted to stand rather than sit during a scene, he would work with you. What was impressive about him was that he loved to work with actors, and he made you feel safe because you believed in his vision. He hired you as an actor because he truly believed in you.

ALEX HALEY AND NORMAN LEAR

Playing that role gave me an opportunity to show other sides of my acting ability. I was seen by many casting directors as the big, tall, angry black man. I wanted to show that I could be more than that. The character of Leon was a soft-spoken brilliant sociopathic businessman, and I wanted the opportunity to let casting directors know that I had more range. One of my favorite quotes from that move is, "I never liked you much myself."

Palmerstown, U.S.A. was something that I grew into as an actor. The scripts were great because they really got to the issues of internal family struggles as well as external family experiences in terms of race. The show was without a doubt groundbreaking. We had stars like Louis Gossett Jr., who was the head of the black baseball league. This show enabled me to understand the madness and glory of television acting.

A television series is the hardest work for an actor on the face of this Earth. Why? Because while filming one episode, you have to memorize all the lines for the next episode and be prepared when you step onto the set. You're expected to work ten times harder than you have ever worked in your life. You make good money, but it's either sink or swim. Nobody wants to hear how difficult the monologue is, how long it is, or the fact that you are already working five days this week and don't have time to memorize your lines for the next episode. You work seven days a week as a television series actor. I learned a lot about acting and television and working under grueling conditions. It wasn't easy, but I am so thankful that Norman Lear and Alex Haley let me be a part of their series.

The strange thing is after *Palmerstown* I could not find work as an actor. In those days they had something called a TV Q score, which was a way to measure how familiar audiences were with an actor, TV show, and so forth. If you were on a television show that garnered a lot of publicity, you could be considered "overexposed," which could make it difficult to get hired for another television show or feature because your Q score went down. I did not work for two years. I was so desperate and depressed and angry. Every place I went there was rejection. I thought, *Bill, you know you're a black man in America in Hollywood. You are being delusional. Louis Gossett Jr. won an Academy Award, but how many black men really have an Academy Award? He was an exception. Your black ass better learn how to do more than just act.*

AFI

I was always fascinated by film directing, but I was a coward. I had directed theater, but that entailed a single proscenium, with actors and a set designer and sound, but without all those cables and wires in front hundreds of people and tons of equipment. I always wondered how in the hell they managed all of that. A friend of mine suggested that I apply to the American Film Institute, one of the greatest film schools in the country. I didn't think I would get in, but I was pleasantly surprised when I did. The great Tony Villani was the head of the American Film Institute. My AFI thesis film was called *The Hero*.

Although I was interested in directing, my acting career picked up steam, and I had the opportunity to collaborate with Joel Silver on *Commando*. It was a collaborative effort and we worked together to find the characters. I had never worked with Arnold Schwarzenegger before and found him to be one of the most gracious and kind people in the business. There was no ego trip, just hard work. I really appreciated how I was treated on set. I had never been in a film with that kind of budget before, so to watch it being directed and to see the logistics involved in a production of that size was a real learning experience. There were stunts, stunt doubles, and car crashes. Filming was challenging because there were so many different locations. Mark Lester, the director, was a great visualist. His locations become an integral part of his visual story.

I will never forget having to ride on the back of a garbage truck. A guy we had to assassinate in the film lived in a compound. We tracked him and he took his own trash to the garbage can. So my partner and I waited for him to take his garbage out and then we assassinated him. I had a greater appreciation for garbage collectors after that scene! We rehearsed the big fight scene many, many times. I let Arnold beat me up because I have a kind heart. That movie was an eye-opener for me and a great introduction to Arnold Schwarzenegger and Joel Silver.

PREDATOR

That led to my next role. I had to sit down with that same duo—Joel Silver and Arnold—for *Predator* but it wasn't an audition. During this meeting, they wanted to know my vision of the character. The next day I was hired. I was excited to work with Arnold again because I'd learned a lot from him. In films with Arnold, you have no choice but to fit in because he is a team player. He likes collaboration, respects the other actors on set, and treats them like family. As an actor working alongside Arnold, I never had to deal with ego because he was there doing his job and all he expected me to do was my job.

Predator was made in 1987 and I was working not only with Joel and Arnold, but also Carl Weathers, Jesse Ventura, Shane Black, Sonny Landham, and more. We filmed in the bowels of the jungles of Puerto Vallarta and Palenque, Mexico. Working on *Predator* was an amazing experience. Since I had worked with Arnold and Joel on *Commando* and was invited to join the cast of *Predator*, I appreciated not having to audition after enduring so many rejections. One of the great privileges of working on that movie was watching director John McTiernan again. He has a great ability to work with actors and a unique process for telling a story with the camera. John McTiernan does not move the camera around arbitrarily, he actually uses the camera as a storytelling tool in a brilliant way. When he looks through the lens, he sees a story. So, I learned a lot directorially from him and his focus on the details.

Predator was a new kind of vision for the time as far as action films go. Arnold, Sonny Landham, Jesse Ventura, Carl Weather and all the people there made it a special experience, especially under our working conditions. We shot most scenes in the mountains of Puerto Vallarta, Mexico, a forty-minute drive from the hotel, riding up steep, mountainous terrain with no guardrail on the side. I used to look out the window to see if we were too close to the side of the road because if the driver made a wrong move, we could be over the cliff. Nobody loved that drive, but we made it to and from the set every day. We had small trailers that were more like boxes but they were sufficient. We changed there, but to get food or drink, we went to the catering tent. The caterer was great. He knew how hard we were working and put netting around the tent, but the first few days we were there, we'd get the food with several bugs already in it. The bugs owned the jungle, we were just visitors, and the netting meant nothing to them. They went over it, around it, and under it to get at our food. We complained to the caterer, saying, "We aren't eating this crap; it's got bugs in it." He explained that he was doing the best that he could, but that we were in the middle of a jungle! By the second week, there were still bugs in the food and since that wasn't going to change, we decided to call the bugs "protein."

We were also being trained by a guy who was equipped to show us special forces techniques. He was not brutal but accurate in showing us the things special forces did, things like how to make our movements look authentic, like crawling on our bellies. We were taught concepts as detailed as how to hold our posture with the guns and stealth techniques to stay quiet, so the enemy wouldn't know we were there. We were warned by locals that these jungles had deadly scorpions and coral snakes and that if either stung or bit us, we'd die. And as we were crawling on our stomachs, we could see scorpions *and* coral snakes slithering near our faces as we disrupted their homes. They didn't care about *Predator* the movie; we were invading their space. It was a challenging environment, but we went on in spite of it all.

One of the great things about working on *Predator* was working with Arnold. He carried no ego with him. He was the head of the team and he was a team player. Every morning before reporting to set at 7:30 a.m., Arnold and the rest of the team would get up and run five miles, then come back to the gym. Arnold had full-sized gym equipment and machines shipped to our hotel in Puerto Vallarta, then rented the ballroom at the hotel and turned it into our own personal gym. So, every morning after the five-mile run, we'd come back to the ballroom gym and work out for another hour, eat breakfast, and then go to set. This routine started around 4:00 a.m. I lasted two or three days of this early morning routine because it was exhausting and painful, but those guys were workout freaks. They loved it and made fun of me. I was one of the tallest of the group, but I was the wimp. They caressed me and gave me kisses as a joke, which wasn't the most pleasant, but I deserved some sort of hazing because I should've been working out. It was wonderful. Arnold had a trainer named Schvin, who was even bigger than Arnold. To show his strength, he used to tell Arnold to bend his arms so that his elbows were up against his sides. Then Schvin would stand behind Arnold, put his hands on Arnold's elbows and lift him up and down. It was amazing to see. We all laughed and so did Arnold, but it was an undeniable example of his great strength.

One day, everyone got sick except for me and they were pissed at me. This was during my vegetarian days when I was selective about what I ate. However, despite my diet, the water filtration system at the hotel had broken and the hotel didn't tell us, so I took a shower and then I got just as sick as they were. The cast was gleeful that I had finally gotten sick also. One thing about getting ill in Mexico, things come out of parts of your body all at once and you just had to lay there and take it. It was an adventure for sure.

Next, we traveled to Palenque, near the Guatemalan border. It's like a hidden secret where the Mayan pyramids are. We climbed them and it was amazing to see these structures firsthand. These structures were several stories tall and handcrafted, stone by stone. We were there for what felt like many moons.

Another *Predator* moment that many people find interesting is the fact that the Predator monster, the frightening invincible beast from outer space that appeared in the movie and played by Kevin Peter Hall, was not the Predator as originally conceived. The original Predator was a smaller, more nimble creature that flew through jungle trees with speed and flexibility and fully packed laser guns. He was also invisible and could strike his prey at any time. To create the original Predator, which was not seen in the movie, the actor had to wear a bodysuit made of felt over his entire body, including his head and face. The plan was to insert computer-generated special effects over his body in postproduction, but in order to do this, the Predator had to fly through trees and spin on wires in the humid, sometimes 100-degree weather. The actor had fallen to the ground twice from dehydration and exhaustion, and Joel Silver, under great pressure to meet the production schedule, stated to the actor playing the Predator role, "If you pass out again, I will have to fire you." The actor said, "Joel, I'm not passing out on purpose. I have a bodysuit on. It's 100 degrees with humidity and I'm totally dehydrated." Joel Silver, with as much compassion as he could gather at the moment, had the final say: "I understand the heat. I understand the conditions that we are under. I understand. But if you pass out again, I will have to fire you." Several days went by, and sure enough as the temperature rose, exhaustion and dehydration set in. One day after flying on wires through the trees in the middle of the unforgiving jungle of Puerto Vallarta, Mexico, the actor plopped to the ground again, passed out from exhaustion. At that moment, Joel Silver marched up to him, and as the actor woke up, stated simply, "You're fired." The little-known fact about this true experience is that the actor, that acrobatic, multitalented, martial artist flying through the trees in a felt suit in one of his first jobs in America, was Jean-Claude Van Damme.

We all loved what we accomplished with that film. I remember the night of the *Predator* premiere. Nobody was sure how it was going to turn out because it was different from the typical action film. It was actually an action horror film. However, the risk paid off. It turned out to be a great night and the movie went on to become a huge success thanks to Joel Silver, Arnold Schwarzenegger, and many other great people.

Not long ago, I was at the thirtieth anniversary of *Predator*, and it was spectacular. People gave standing ovations. I didn't realize that *Predator* still had such a big fan base. People expressed their love for the film on many different levels. Arnold reminded me of different challenges that I had forgotten about in terms of the environment that we worked in. When he filmed one of the night scenes that involved the creature, he had to put mud all over his entire body and swim in the cold water. Arnold talked about how that was the most difficult scene to film for him. At that point in the movie, everyone else had been killed except for him and the Predator.

Arnold graciously discussed the brotherhood that we formed on the set because we were so isolated. We relied on each other as we faced various challenges in the jungle. In a scene with actor Sonny Landham, Arnold even got bit by a scorpion and was rushed to the hospital. Jesse Ventura and I stayed in touch for years after the film, and he talked about his political points of view. Arnold and I have been in touch on and off throughout the years. Being at that event was great, and seeing the respect people have for *Predator* was encouraging.

It's all about relationships in the industry. My next movie, *Action Jackson*, starred one of my *Predator* costars and was produced by Joel Silver. It was an updated take on the blaxploitation movies of the 1970s, starring Carl Weathers and singer and actress Vanity. It even had music by the Pointer Sisters (who were in *Car Wash* with me) and another of my favorites, Herbie Hancock.

ACTION JACKSON

With Sharon Stone and Vanity on the set, the male crew members were obviously excited about filming. When Carl Weathers and I had scenes together, the crew was rarely present. For some miraculous reason, whenever

Sharon or Vanity did a scene, teamsters, electricians, and other crew showed up on set. I don't think they knew what those scenes were about, but they didn't want to miss them.

That movie was tough for me personally because while filming, my father died. I had to go back to Poughkeepsie, New York, for his funeral and to take care of my family. This totally disrupted the shooting schedule, but the crew, cast, and studio were gracious and kind to me. They told me to get back as soon as I could but advised me not to rush. They had my back. Carl made sure that everything was taken care of, and we have remained friends ever since.

MEL GIBSON

I worked with Mel Gibson on two films, the action movie *Payback* and the comedy *Bird on a Wire* with Goldie Hawn. I was excited because Mel was one of my favorite actors and directors. He was loved by his fans. On the set of *Payback*, his trailer was not far from mine. One day, we were called to set for a scene. Mel came out of his trailer and was immediately surrounded by fans to the extent that security had to clear the way for him to make it to set. He didn't mind shaking some hands and signing a few autographs, but he didn't really like it when a couple hundred people would show up.

Goldie and Mel were hilarious on the set of *Bird on a Wire*, filmed in Vancouver. They would joke with each other often. One of my biggest scenes in the film was scheduled for a Monday. The weekend before the scene, I flew a girlfriend of mine in from Los Angeles. That Sunday night, we both drank and partied and smoked a joint that she had gotten into Canada by stuffing the marijuana inside her. I know I shouldn't have done it, but I smoked some of it. I was supposed to be on set early in the morning but didn't get to sleep until a couple of hours before the shoot. I had memorized my lines, but when the cameras started rolling and the director called action, my mind went blank. For some reason, I could not remember my lines for the entire scene, not a single word. After twelve takes, director John Badham yelled cut. He had the script supervisor print out the words for the scene large enough so that I could use them as cue cards as she stood to the right of the camera. I barely made it through that even with the cue cards. John was pissed, as he should have been. Even though I apologized to him on set, in person, he never forgave me because I cost him time and money. That was one of the low moments in my career and I never repeated that pattern again.

TERRENCE HOWARD

I had the privilege of working with Terrence Howard and 50 Cent on *Get Rich or Die Tryin'*. Terrence was always prepared. One of the most powerful aspects of his talent as an actor is his ability to listen whether you have dialogue with him or not. He listens to everything you have to say. He was never there just to do his lines.

Ironically, I had worked with his grandmother, Minnie Gentry, on Broadway. As a young actor, I used to stand in the wings and watch her perform. It was like watching an acting teacher showing you the ins and outs of acting. *Ain't Suppose to Die a Natural Death* was a Melvin Van Peebles play on Broadway directed by my friend from school, Gilbert Moses. Minnie Gentry closed the show with a monologue to the audience called "I Put a Spell on You." She played the role of a witch doctor who threw her hands, her cane, and her wand, addressing the mostly white audience directly. When she said, "I put a spell on you. . . . I hope your children end up drug addicts, too," it made white audiences uncomfortable.

As she went on with the monologue, she would wish that the hardship and plight of the black community would visit the doors of every white person in the audience. She was dressed in rags like an homeless street woman, but her power and passion resulted in a standing ovation every evening as she took her bow. Minnie Gentry was one of the best actresses that I've ever had the privilege of working with. So working with Terrence on *Get Rich or Die Tryin'* was a continuation of my experience with that family.

One day I called Terrence and asked him to come by my home because I had a gift for him. I gave him a poster that I had saved and framed of *Ain't Supposed to Die a Natural Death*, which he graciously accepted. Working with 50 Cent on the film was a revelatory experience, too. I had known him only through his music as a shirtless rapper/gangster, an inarticulate street thug, but when I met him and spoke to him, he was the total opposite. He was a well-spoken, talented, brilliant businessman. We had many conversations on set about the business of the industry, and his success speaks for itself.

X-MEN

The blockbuster *X-Men* was the first time I worked on a movie using green screen. As actors, we had to look at and talk to a screen as if we were seeing rocket ships, battles, and other fantastical things. There were no rocket ships or battles in sight, but we had to act based on what our character would be seeing in the movie. It was challenging for me because I was used to working with actors face-to-face, eye to eye, but you have to bring something extra to the party if you are working with green screen. It takes time to get over the fact that there is no real person there to talk to. It also forces you to go more deeply into the character. When I saw the film cut together, I was amazed by the brilliance of the visual effects and computer-generated images. It was seamless and well edited.

MENACE II SOCIETY

Of all the movies that I have been in, the one that gets me the most feedback, whether I recognize it as my best performance or not, is *Menace II Society*. No matter where I go around the world, people always say the same line: "You know you done fucked up, right?" I have no idea why that caught on, but it did. Maybe it was the intimidation of a young man trying to pull one over on me, but whatever it was, it stuck in people's minds.

Menace II Society showed the truth about and perspective of our young black men. It showed that they are real people with limited life choices. In the film, they made some bad choices, whether it was robbing, murdering, selling drugs, taking drugs, or being in a street gang. The film talks about the dilemma that young black men in this nation face. What options do they really have in certain family situations, financial situations, and neighborhoods? I am not making excuses for them, but I will say that if you research low-income black communities, a lot of our young men as depicted in the film are living in households that are not conducive to raising a child, especially a teen. These are households with parents hooked on illegal substances or fathers not in the home. You have fourteen or fifteen-year-old "men of the house" taking care of younger siblings while their mother is hooked on heroin or never home because she's working two jobs to make the rent on time.

As a result, a lot of these young men join gangs and sell drugs to bring money into the household. Many times young black men who have made terrible decisions are perceived as innately evil and stupid, but a lot of these young men are "potential businessmen" who would never otherwise get real-world business opportunities. They are guilty until proven innocent and their living conditions provide a direct pathway to prison. There are kids graduating with second-grade reading levels. How do you survive in a global economy with a limited education? You don't. I'm not suggesting that there is no responsibility on their part, but we have to recognize how many things are stacked against them. The odds are never on their side. The resources to uplift the young men in these communities are not there, and many times there is no support at home.

Menace II Society was an insightful experience for me in many ways. My contribution to the film appears to be minor when judged by the number of my lines, but I had one line that resonated. "You know you done fucked up, right?" is a line that young people can relate to because they have been in similar situations. Now I hear it and see it online in memes and GIFs everywhere. It just goes to show how pivotal and impactful that film was, particularly to the black community.

HOMELESS

Nobody ever really cares
That
A bird has wings
As long as it flies
As
Long

As it dips
And swoops
And sings
Nobody really cares
Nobody ever really cares
Whether
A
Flower grows
As long
As it doesn't
Develop a nose
As long
As
A rose
Is
A rose
Is
A rose
That
Throws us kisses
When
A
Soft breeze blows
Nobody really cares
Nobody seems to really care
About the other's pain
For we
Must laugh
And dance
And sing
And not remind us
Of
Anything
That
Resembles fears
That

We've
Secretly tried to cover
By
Pretending
To be
Devoted lovers
Of
Everything
Except
Ourselves
Just
Bridges
Made
Of
Oyster shells
So
When
The bridge collapses
And
You fall
And
Break
On
Velvet blue concrete
You thought
Was
A lake
Just
Chalk it up
As
Another mistake
Because
Nobody
Really
Cares

CANCER

Although I was doing great in my professional life, there was a personal challenge that threatened to derail my progress. I was diagnosed with prostate cancer in 1994. When the doctor told me that I had cancer, I automatically thought I was dying and that my body had betrayed me. I thought, *What did I do to deserve this? Why is my body doing this to me?* I spent a lot of time by myself, in silence, sometimes for days. When I went back to the doctor, he said I needed surgery to remove the cancer. Fortunately, the woman I was seeing at the time realized how terrified I was. She suggested that I do some more research about my diagnosis. She let me know that there were doctors who dealt specifically with cancer. I never knew what an oncologist was until I researched prostate cancer. I discovered different treatment options and learned that not everybody dies from cancer but that black men are the number-one victims of prostate cancer because fewer black men get their prostate checked.

After all this research I decided to explore different surgeons, radiologists, and oncologists. I found an oncologist named Dr. Mark Schultz. The Prostate Oncology Center was one of the most advanced prostate centers in the country, and Dr. Schultz was on the pioneering edge of this research. He had great relationships with surgeons, radiologists, and other cancer professionals. He also said something to me that was very important: "Bill, no matter what anybody says, you are in charge of your own life." He informed me there was an option aside from surgery and radiation called watchful waiting, during which you change your diet and exercise patterns and get your prostate-specific antigen checked every few months to determine what the next steps should be. Watchful waiting seemed like the best option for me because I was terrified of the idea of surgery—I don't like needles or hospitals. So I went with watchful waiting. I changed my diet and my exercise plan while getting checked every three months. I got deeper into my meditation and started some alternative treatments like acupuncture, acupressure, and other things.

I had no operations, but in 2015, my other oncologist, Dr. Duke Vaughn, spotted something on my prostate. He informed me it was not life threatening but it needed to be taken care of. He suggested freezing that part of my prostate and getting rid of it that way. So I had that procedure done and it was successful. Having cancer does something to your personal life, because you have to have a discussion with whomever you're involved with, telling them what is going on. That cuts off a lot of relationships no matter how gently you do it. It impacts your entire life and how you function. Finding someone who loves you unconditionally is not easy, and if you're considered "sick" in this industry, you're seen as a pariah. A lot of friends feel sorry for you and call you three times a day, which is appreciated, but when everyone treats you like you're going to die—and some like you are already dead—it's a lot to handle.

When I first found out I had cancer, I did think I was going to die. I thought it was over. Cancer is a disease that kills, but at the same time through God's graces, you can recover and heal from it in a number of different ways. When it comes to prostate cancer, you should consider and understand all the options. Don't just go to just one doctor. Get multiple opinions. You have to do the research on your own. As a black man I've been very skeptical about hospitals and medicine, but my brothers of all races, forget about the mistrust for second and think about the life-saving grace of catching this issue early. There is hope.

AND GODS WORE SHADES

Claude Collummbbuuss
Came again
Today
And everyone
Ran
To get
Their
Spears
And
Shields
Mothers
Took babies

From baskets
Children
Ran to huts
For razors
Allllll sheep
Were
Herded down the hill
And
There was no
Welcome to our land
No
Welcome hand
No one
Talked of even trades
Blood
Was
Poured from pitchers
And gods wore shades

Chapter 14

DIRECTING HOLLYWOOD

If a man does not seek humility, humility will seek the man.—Unknown

PRIME-TIME SERIAL DRAMAS, CALLED "SOAP OPERAS" by many people, were very popular in the late 1970s through the 1980s. One of the most popular and longest running was *Knots Landing*, a spin-off of another highly rated TV show called *Dallas*. I was new to directing, and I had the opportunity to direct *Knots Landing* due to a mistake in which the executive producer mixed up my submission tape with someone else's. I knew how difficult television was as an actor, and I found out that it's a real challenge as a director, too. You have seven days to prep and seven days to shoot each show. Most shows are an hour long, and you must know the script locations, the blocking, and the episodes prior to your episode. The style of the show already has been established and you're expected to maintain that style. Within that context, they are also looking for what you can bring to a show, whether it be nuance or innovation. Creativity and artistic freedom are limited because you're stepping into a family that has established itself already. This is where you learn a lot about the difference between the film and television genres.

As a director for television, you sit by the editor, who is the editor for the entire show, not just your episode. In feature films you get sometimes three months, but in TV, it's just fourteen days, seven days for preproduction and seven days to shoot. To be able to direct something within that time frame is an exercise in discipline. Established, well-known directors typically take Christmas, Thanksgiving, and other holidays off to vacation with their families. When I first started as a young black director, I didn't want to take any days off because I did not want to risk not working. I needed as much exposure as possible, so my holidays were spent filming. I offered to take the work schedules that others didn't want. I learned how to manage time and how to get all my shots completed within the allotted window. The right hand of the director is usually the first assistant director, or AD, and I would divide each scene down to the second to make sure we did not go over our time. The amount of time I had to shoot the scene determined the number of shots I could put together to tell a story visually. It takes incredible discipline to direct television. It's really a family of people working together to get the job done in the time that is given, and it is never, ever easy. Network television is probably the most challenging directing jobs that I have experienced. Many people say independent movies are more difficult, but there is still more time to shoot them than with television. That time crunch is nonnegotiable.

I was one of the first black men in many entertainment positions—directing, acting, and producing—at a time when Hollywood was not accustomed to seeing black men in charge. I followed in the footsteps of Michael Schultz, Gordon Parks, Sidney Poitier, and others, but it wasn't an easy journey by any means.

DALLAS

My first day on the set of *Dallas* was invigorating and terrifying simultaneously. One of the most successful and popular shows in the history of television—which had never had a black director—invited me to direct episodes. I was very excited about the opportunity. The show had actors like Larry Hagman, Patrick Duffy, Linda Gray, Ken Kercheval, and Barbara Bel Geddes. When I walked onto the set I was overwhelmed because it was intimidating. First, I directed a couple of scenes that did not include Larry Hagman. When Larry came to the set, he greeted me with open arms.

He shook my hand, looked me in my eye, and said, "Welcome to *Dallas*. You and I are going to get along fine if every day you have me out of here by 2:00. Is that a problem?"

I assured him that would be the case. What else could I say to J. R. Ewing? He shook my hand. He lived far away so he wanted to get out early to make the commute home. The other actors were gracious and supportive of me, too. The show was well established when I started directing. It was a well-oiled machine. As long as I followed the template of the show, stayed on budget and on time, and had Larry Hagman out by 2:00, I didn't have any problems. Entering a show that is already established creatively is complex because you have to be inventive within the confines of the previously designed context. The look and style of the show have been established from blocking, camera moves, and angles. Yes, every script is different, but there is an established format.

The same applied to the other serial TV dramas I directed including *Knots Landing* and *Falcon Crest*. They were both the same in that as long as you understand the business of shooting a series as a director, you would be fine. The creative process was already established, but what many episodic shows look for is the director's ability to manage time, people, and money. You have a certain number of scenes per day, which breaks down to the number of setups. Along with the first AD and director of photography (DP), you determine how long each setup will take and how much time will be needed to complete each scene. Within a twelve-hour period, you have to complete the entire day's work. No matter who the stars are, you have to make sure they get to set on time, communicate in a way that makes them feel comfortable, and gain their trust. In terms of money, you cannot go over time, you can never ignore that budget, because they are not giving you extra money to shoot anything. They expect you to know coming in the business of episodic television. Finally, they must like you. It's like going to an event. If the people throwing the event find you annoying, they will not invite you back again.

PLANE CRASH

In 1984, I had been working as a director for a number of years and had some great television success. As a black man in the industry, I was fortunate to be working and took every job I could get because I never knew how long it was going to last. As a result, I learned a great deal about structure, scheduling, and managing people, money, and time. I was exhausted from working on various shows and movies when my agent told me to take a vacation. Agents get 10 percent of what you make, so for an agent to tell you to take some time off meant that their investment—me, in this case—looked like it wasn't going to be able to bring in the money. I was grateful for my success, but I was not doing well physically or psychologically. So I decided to go to Hawaii for the first time, and I decided to go alone. I didn't want to take anyone with me because I wanted to be able to just relax and reflect on clarity.

Hawaii was like heaven on Earth. The landscape was beautiful, and the people were kind. I was having a great time and one of the hotel staffers suggested I visit the other islands because I had never been to Hawaii. I went to the lobby and they had something called Panorama Tours, or island-hopper tours. So, I went on the island-hopper Panorama Tours. We went from the big island to some smaller islands. Once we landed, they gave us a grand tour of the lava rocks and great scenery. While in Maui, I met a beautiful young woman whom I was trying to impress. To show how corny I am, I bought two packs of macadamia nuts and shared them with her when we got back on the plane.

As we were chatting, laughing, and recapping the great tour, the plane started shaking. It was a twin-engine plane with eleven or twelve passengers, including the pilot. When the plane started shaking, everyone froze, but then there was a sigh of relief because everything seemed to be fine. The lady and I continued chatting and enjoying the macadamia nuts until the plane started shaking violently again. The pilot told everyone to go to their seats. We sat down. In the movies, when the plane is in trouble, you usually hear the pilot tell everyone to stay calm and that they have everything under control, but the pilot on our plane said no such thing. He frantically flipped switches and pressed buttons and then said, "Help us Jesus. Help us Mary. Help us Lord." That was not encouraging. As I looked out the window, I thought we were really close to the—BAM! Before I could finish my thought, we hit the water. You would think the water would be soft, but when you hit water from a certain height, it's not soft at all. It's like hitting concrete. The pilot saved our lives because the tail of the plane hit first. If the front of the plane hit first, there would have been no survivors. When the nose of the plane hit the water, it tore the seats out of the floor and threw us forward. My face hit the back of the seat in front of me and split the top of my nose.

At that moment, I was knocked out physically, but I had an out-of-body experience. My awareness and consciousness rose up above me and the others in the plane and observed the chaotic scene. I was looking down at the bleeding body in my seat and at all the people screaming as the water rose. The pilot's face had struck the instrument panel and he was groggy. The observer—or whatever you want to call it—was totally calm and continued objectively observing. The plane is sinking at that point. When I regained my senses, I shook my head back into full consciousness and saw blood, water rising, and the chaos of everything around me. I said out loud, "Bill, you always wanted to know how you were going to die and now you know." I said this because I don't swim, remember, and the water was rising in the plane.

The pilot got up, opened the emergency exit door, and screamed, "Everybody out of the plane! Get out now!" and instructed us how to put on our life vests. People were following instructions except for me and another woman who was unconscious. The pilot looked at me and said, "You! The life vest is under your seat!" I got the vest from under my seat and put it on. The pilot instructed us to go to the wing of the plane. I stopped when I got there. The pilot said, "Pull the strings to inflate." I looked down at what looked like a thousand strings and started pulling, but nothing happened. The pilot approached me and pulled the correct string to inflate my vest, then jumped off the wing and into the water, leaving me alone on the wing.

From the water, the pilot yelled, "Jump. Undertow. Jump. Undertow!" By this point, all but one passenger and I had made it off the plane. "I don't know how to swim!" I said. He repeated, "Jump! Undertow." I jumped in the water only to find out I hadn't strapped the vest around my waist. I went down once in the water. Twice. After I popped up the third time, the life vest was right by my head. I put it around my neck, fastened it, and doggy paddled away. As I was paddling around, I reached an older man without a life vest. He asked to hang on to mine and that was fine by me. I figured if we were all going to die, we might as well be cooperative. From a few hundred feet away, I looked over at the plane just in time to see water swallow the entire thing with the unconscious woman still inside.

Out of nowhere a lady screamed, "Boats! Planes! Boats! Planes!" People ask me if I believe in God and I say, "No, I don't just *believe* in God. I *know* God exists and I will tell you why." There is one reason. I thought these were delusional visions that happen just before you die. I thought that just before you die, you see all the things you want to happen. I was sure we were going to get eaten by sharks that smelled our blood in the water, but the lady kept repeating, "Boats. Planes. Boats. Planes." This is where it got real interesting.

Twice a year, the Hawaii Fire Department does emergency maneuvers in different parts of the ocean to practice rescue missions. On that day, they were a mile and a half away and saw the plane go down. I ask anyone reading this to take those odds to Vegas. What are the odds of the plane crashing near the Hawaii Fire Department's emergency rescue exercises? There is only one explanation: God. I was put in the boat with the other passengers and we were given blankets to drape over our shivering bodies. The rescuers dove into the water and rescued the woman trapped in her seat. Miraculously, nobody died in the crash.

On the way back to shore, the pale, tall, thin, white pilot with blue eyes—an Ichabod Crane type who had saved my life—was in the same boat as me. We both shivered under our blankets. I said, "Sir, thank you for saving my life because I was in shock and don't know how to swim. You inflated my life vest and got me off that plane. Thanks to you I am here."

He replied, "I appreciate what you just said, but I am Catholic and I believe in Jesus Christ. I don't know who you pray to, but if you do pray and believe, don't thank me. Thank that." Then he turned away from me, grabbed my shoulder, looked back at my face, and started crying like baby. Tears flowed from both of our eyes. It was a "God moment" because I knew it wasn't the pilot or me that saved my life; it was something far beyond my intellect, reason, or anything I could imagine. I was changed after that.

We reached shore and ambulances were waiting there to take us to the hospital. They looked us over, in shock that we all had survived the crash. When I went to the hospital, I was in shock for a few days. I called my family and told them what happened. They were horrified. I grew up Baptist but until that day I put God in a box. I only talked to God when I went to church on Sunday, but God was not in the church that day. God was in Hawaii in the ocean with eleven others and me. That day God jumped out of the box of my definitions. God was something far beyond my imagination, ego, and intellect. God was something I could not define but I knew deep in my soul He existed and there were things that God had in store for me. I pray in my soul that I am doing at least some of what the God of the universe expects me to do.

A RAGE IN HARLEM

Not one to slow down, once I returned, it was back to business, taking jobs and working with gusto. After that near-death experience, it was like I was rejuvenated. I was determined to continue building my career. My first real directing gig that got some attention was *A Rage in Harlem* starring Forest Whitaker, Gregory Hines, Robin Givens, and Badja Djola. We filmed in Cincinnati, Ohio. It was based on a Chester Himes novel, and when it was offered to me, I really wanted to put this film together because it had comedy and wit. It also dealt with love and survival challenges. The main character, played by Forest, was a nerdy guy who didn't know much about women but ended up being the hero.

Badja Djola, who played Robin Givens's pimp, was a great actor and did a wonderful job. He was subtle but effective. I remember the first scene that Robin Givens and Baja Djola did together. It was a bedroom scene, which is always challenging. Her character hated him, but at the same time she was terrified because she knew he would kill her if it came down to it. When she first met Jackson, played by Forest, she thought he was her salvation from her pimp. She ended up really liking Jackson because he was the first man who treated her with respect. There was an innocence about their care for one another.

I was so proud to be a part of this film, especially because it was based on the Chester Himes novel. Chester wrote many great books that I enjoyed. Being in Cincinnati at that time with a lot of night shoots was not the easiest thing to do. I had a great DP and AD, but there were a lot of five- and six-day workweeks, and the many night shoots made it totally exhausting. Some nights, due to great planning, we were able to get through many of the most difficult scenes. Overall, we had to shoot a lot in a short period of time. Thank God we had a great cast and crew.

Good directors have to be creative people. We are able to read a script and come up with ideas on how to shoot each scene. We talk to the actors about their perception of the character and collaborate with all departments to achieve the overall vision. Directors talk to the prop master, production designer, costume designer, director of photography, first assistant director, and many others. After the vision is communicated to every department, the director must manage time, people, and money.

I was prepared for this film because of my experience directing *The Killing Floor*, my first film shot in Chicago, and because I had directed television, and learning to work in that fast-paced environment is great training. There are only twenty-four hours in a day. You have twelve hours to shoot, but you have to account for an hour lunch and other crew breaks in there. How do you finish the day? Every second of every day needs to be scheduled, because the more you wait, the more it costs the production money, and you do not work if you cost the production more money. I had to be very disciplined in terms of budgets, time, and people. It taught me how to hire people who can get the job done, which did not always mean hiring my buddies. That was a difficult lesson to learn. Overall, you had to have the best of the best because it is your reputation on the line. The studio will not blame your friends, they will blame you. I learned quickly how to manage time, people, and money, which became the foundation of my career, and one of the reasons I have worked continuously for so long.

Tony Vilani from the American Film Institute always talked about the business of this industry, and he helped me focus on that when I shot my AFI thesis film, *The Hero*. I think many people don't understand that directors are also managers. So, *A Rage in Harlem* was challenging because we had a low budget and little time. Once I agreed to the budget and schedule, that's all the studio wanted to hear. No excuses. We faced many challenges, especially during the night, since there are so many uncontrollable aspects. Working with Forest Whitaker was a dream. He is a wonderful and fearless actor who always gives you his all. Robin Givens is another great human being who can do anything from Shakespeare to playing a prostitute. Danny Glover, who was also in the film, has been a friend for many years. He's not only a wonderful actor but a great human being, entrepreneur, and activist. When he feels there is a just cause, he is willing to make sacrifices and be involved with his community. He has his own theater company and does a lot of stage plays. Danny always has stood up for what he believes in. Some of his opinions may not be popular, but he does not let that keep him quiet. He stays true to what he believes in and what he cares for.

Badja Djola was an amazing actor as well. He did not say much but when he did, it got your attention. He had a deep baritone voice with looks and posture that sold his role. He was someone I looked forward to working with again, but unfortunately, he was another who died too early, at age fifty-six, of a heart attack in 2005. We loved him, and his spirit and talents will always be with us. *A Rage in Harlem* was a film I was passionate about because it had music and even a dance with Little Richard. Working with that team of people was an unforgettable blessing. The movie was ultimately a success because it made its money back, which is crucial in this business.

THE CEMETERY CLUB

Directing *The Cemetery Club* was interesting because the cast was made up mostly of women, with Ellen Burstyn, Olympia Dukakis, and Diane Ladd. It was a great collaborative experience. Before it was a film, *The Cemetery Club* was a successful off-Broadway play. We all worked hard adapting it for the screen. It was about three women whose husbands had passed away who came together to create what they called "The Cemetery Club" to give each other mutual support in moving forward with their lives. What I loved about the film and the script was its humanity. We are all going to die, and how we handle it—not only our own death, but the deaths of those around us—is heart-wrenchingly challenging.

I had a special connection to one of the actresses because I attended the Tisch School of the Arts at NYU, where one of my teachers was Olympia Dukakis. She taught me acting techniques and how to deal with actors. So we would laugh at the fact that I was directing my acting teacher. Watching these three strong actresses dig into their souls to portray lost and mourning women was inspiring to watch. It was fascinating to learn how some people choose to deal with their pain. *The Cemetery Club* was also the first Disney film I directed.

WHOOPI GOLDBERG

My second Disney film was a sequel to the major hit *Sister Act*. Disney kindly considered me to direct *Sister Act 2: Back in the Habit*. I had the good fortune of working with some of the great talents in the industry: Whoopi Goldberg, Lauryn Hill, Sheryl Lee Ralph, Maggie Smith, Jennifer Love Hewitt, Monica Calhoun, and Ryan Toby.

Whoopi was a joy to work with. She worked hard. She did a lot of improvisation during filming. Sometimes it was better than what was scripted. The studio was not always happy about this, but they allowed her freedom to execute the character in the way she saw fit. The scene in the film where Whoopi's students put glue on her chair was one of the funniest scenes in the movie. From the moment when she first discovered that she could not get up from the chair to her exit from the classroom by rolling down the hallway in it was improvised. It created true laughter from the cast and crew on set.

Working with the talented vocalist and rapper Lauryn Hill was a privilege. She had not yet recorded her historic album *The Miseducation of Lauryn Hill*. Lauryn was one of the first females in the industry to be at the top of her game in all three categories—rapping, acting, and singing. Like Whoopi, she gave 1,000 percent on set.

Some of my favorite scenes in the film were the mother-daughter interactions between Sheryl Lee Ralph and Lauryn Hill. Sheryl was a mother who wanted to protect her daughter, but Lauryn played a daughter who wanted to freely live out her spiritual desires. Whoopi Goldberg gives Lauryn Hill's character a book entitled *Letters to a Young Poet* by Rainer Maria Rilke. In that scene, Whoopi's character tells the young student to read the book because it changed her life. The book tells young people to follow their dreams, no matter what anybody else says.

The scene with the song "His Eye Is on the Sparrow" is another one of my favorite scenes. It features a duet between Lauryn's character and her classmate played by Tanya Blount. In rehearsals and during filming, the power of that scene was based not only the music, but those two great voices that made you feel the spirit they were singing about.

Working with choreographers Michael Peters and Otis Sallid was a great experience because they both knew how to use movement to tell the story. The concluding musical number "Joyful Joyful" was the climax of the film. The theme of the movie was powerful. Religion and faith could bring people of different ages, genders, and ethnicities together for one purpose and one cause: to appreciate each other's existence and to respect what each person brings to the party because we have our humanity in common.

When I was hired to direct *Sister Act 2*, I was conflicted. *Sister Act* had been so successful and had a major audience, and if the sequel did not meet this high standard, my career would have been negatively impacted. I was encouraged by the fact that it was a musical. I had always wanted to direct a musical. Being able to work with Whoopi Goldberg and the other cast members also interested me. These encouragements overcame my fears. I was determined to make it the best work I had done to that point. I think people don't understand the amount of work that is put into choreographing major musical numbers. You have to work with the dancers, musicians, and choreographer. There were hours and days of rehearsal, rehearsal, rehearsal. You have to be sure that the number does not stop the show, but instead moves the story along. When it all comes together, and you watch the audience feel the experience, it's all worth it.

HOODLUM

In late 1996, I directed a film entitled *Hoodlum*. It starred Laurence Fishburne, Cicely Tyson, Tim Roth, Vanessa Williams, Andy Garcia, J. W. Smith, Paul Benjamin, Chi McBride, Loretta Devine, Clarence Williams III, Queen Latifah, and John Toles-Bey. *Hoodlum* tracks the life of Madame Queen, played by Cicely, and her protégé, Bumpy Johnson, played by Laurence. Madame Q ran the numbers game in 1930s Harlem. She and Bumpy Johnson fought with the Italian mafia over control of the numbers game in Harlem. Including preproduction and production, we spent several months in Chicago working, drinking, and partying at blues clubs, working and partying at jazz clubs, and eating pigs feet, mustard greens, potato salad, and some of the best barbeque I'd ever tasted in my life.

We shot under difficult conditions due to time limitations, but I had the great pleasure of working with some of the best actors of that period.

Laurence is the ultimate professional who prepares for every role in detail. He's a collaborative actor who wants to make his performance better no matter how good you say it is. The beautiful and gracious Vanessa Williams played the part of Bumpy Johnson's lady and would always ask, "Do you want something different?" or "Do you want more?" She was always open to suggestion, as was Queen Latifah.

One of the greatest incidents was with Andy Garcia, who played the part of Lucky Luciano. Andy is a perfectionist in the details of each character that he plays. Lucky had a saggy, lazy eye that was permanently half-closed. For months before we started production, Andy Garcia was searching for ways to create that eye effect without piling on tons of makeup and special effects. One day when he was sitting in front of a mirror for makeup, he saw a container with transparent tape, ripped off a piece and put it over his eyelid so that he could not completely open or close the eye. He had the makeup artist put makeup on top of the tape, and that's how Andy Garcia got his saggy, lazy eye as Lucky Luciano.

On the last day of shooting, we had to be finished, though we were already a half-day behind schedule. We were given a deadline that we couldn't miss, so we shot for an entire day and into the night until the next morning. We were shooting the bathroom scene where Bumpy Johnson (Laurence Fishburne) and Francine (Vanessa Williams) are attacked by two mob members. We had been working for twenty consecutive hours by the time we got to this scene and everyone was exhausted. Someone, after a take that went wrong, made the mistake of laughing. To this day I cannot tell you who it came from or why, but that laughter started with one crew member and spread through the entire crew and cast, and we did not stop laughing for fifteen minutes. When I say laughing, I mean crawling—not chuckles, not giggles—but crawling-on-the-floor hysteria due to exhaustion. After we finished laughing, we took a ten-minute break and started filming again. It was a moment of simultaneous joy, exhaustion, and humanity. We were a family and it was one of the most rewarding experiences of my directing career.

Laurence and I worked on another film that I directed, *Deep Cover*. As I said, Laurence is fearless as an actor who will take on any role that he truly believes in, something many actors will not do. Most actors stick to a character type or niche because they feel safe there. Laurence does not really have a character type. He has done Broadway plays, off-Broadway plays, films, and television. He does dramas, supernatural hero flicks, and comedies. He commits 1,000 percent to the moment and what the director has asked him to do. He surrenders himself to every role.

In *Deep Cover*, Laurence's character is an undercover agent partnered with Jeff Goldblum's character, who doesn't know he's an undercover agent. Clarence Williams III is an officer who is aware of the undercover agent, confronts Jeff Goldblum in the parking lot, and gets shot. Clarence and Laurence are on the same side, working to keep drugs off the street. If you watch the movie, you'll see something happen to Laurence's character when Jeff's character shoots Clarence's character: his humanity shatters in front of your eyes as he rushes to Clarence, who is dying in his arms. He looks with tears not in his eyes but tears in the voice from his soul when he says, "Oh, you shouldn't have done that." At first it starts out as pain, but he keeps repeating this line and that pain turns to anger, and that anger turns to rage, and he kills Jeff Goldblum's character on the spot. It was one of the most powerful moments in *Deep Cover*, and the truth of the moment is so compelling that you feel it.

FOREST WHITAKER AND OSSIE DAVIS

Deacons for Defense, which starred Forest Whitaker, Ossie Davis, Chris Britton, and Jonathon Silverman, was based on the true story of black men from the South who came back from the war and faced racism, ignorance, and stupidity. They fought for this nation and believed in this nation but came back from war only to fight for their basic human rights. At some point, they got tired. They got tired of seeing their children and wives being humiliated and assaulted. They just got tired. So one day they came together to do something about it. One of them said that if they attack one of us, they attack all of us, and there will be consequences. Once the white community found out about them coming together, they were terrified. The black men never went after a white person to hurt him but simply to defend their families and their homes. Because they refused to back down, these men were assaulted and their houses were burned. In spite of all this hatred, they continued to defend their families.

When I first heard the story, I was compelled. What I later learned was they had also acted like the Secret Service for people like Dr. Martin Luther King Jr and others. They were adept at staying out of sight while providing protection. When Dr. King marched, these "deacons for defense" were there. When Dr. King spoke, they were watching out for him. They had his back when he came to the South. I wanted to direct this film because I wanted to show black people coming together for the good of the black community. They stood up to the tyranny of the lynchings and beatings. They got sick and tired of being sick and tired. They really wanted to be able to leave a legacy for their children.

Working with the great Ossie Davis was so memorable. We used to go to dinner and talk about the industry. We talked about when he first started, what it was like being one of the only black men in this industry, and how he handled the racism. We even talked about how he and his wife became big stage actors. He told me some amazing stories. He never bragged, and he didn't have a big ego. He was a great human being with a great spirit and integrity. Hollywood had shaped him into a person with scars but also with pride and resistance. He had an elegance that was unmatched.

The message of *Deacons for Defense* was something I wanted to get out there because I felt it was important to see the behind-the-scenes heroes of the civil rights movement who stood up for themselves and for their culture.

COVER

The movie *Cover* was one of my great passion projects because it was based on an experience of one of my goddaughters. This goddaughter is smart, beautiful, and talented. She was happily married. One day she wasn't feeling well and went to the doctor. They did tests to see what was wrong. When the test results came back a few days later, the doctor called her in to the office. The doctor revealed to her in person that she was HIV positive. She couldn't believe it because she had been married for a number of years and never had an affair with anyone. She was in complete shock. She went to her husband and told him that she was HIV positive. His response was "Who have you been sleeping with?" This enraged her, and it was not a pretty situation. For a long time, she was destroyed by this. She did research and got second opinions. It was devastating, but her husband never admitted anything. He suggested that it could have come from a blood transfusion that she never knew about. None of his excuses made any sense.

Two things happened to her. First, her self-esteem dropped to the point where she stayed in the relationship and for a year was totally destroyed. She didn't leave the house because she felt distraught. At one point she decided to be proactive. She had someone follow her husband and discovered he was seeing another man. This affair has been going on for years. Even though he married her, he was still seeing his mister. When she confronted him with the evidence, he was outraged that she had spied on him.

A couple of weeks later, she received a phone call from the other man who said, "Bitch, you know you are living in my house, right? He has you as a front, but I'm the person he loves." He hung up. That was the foundation of their separation. I created the film because I love women and I value honesty in a relationship. I wanted to make a film to help women understand that what they see is not always what they get. It's not right what he did, but it is vital to understand everything about a person and to get tested before marriage. It's important to know the signs of betrayal and hypocrisy. Not that you should be suspicious of everybody, but you should be aware of the signs.

It was great working with Aunjanue Ellis, Razaaq Adoti, Vivica A. Fox, Leon, Louis Gossett Jr., Obba Babatundé, Kenya Cagle, Lorenzo Raybon, and Patti LaBelle. We had a very low budget. It's funny now, but in the middle of filming, the producer came to me and said we ran out of money and that he had to shut the film down. I had to deliver the message to the cast and crew, which was not fun. We shut down production for a couple of weeks. The grips ran off with the equipment and some of the film we shot because they weren't paid. It was a horrible experience. We stayed in hotels in Philly and I had to sneak past the front desk or go out the back way because they wanted payment for the room. It was a nightmare and one of the more challenging experiences. Corey Redman, the executive producer, went to L.A. and got some more funding to finish the film. We were supposed to release it with Fox, but our Fox contract expired before the film was finished. So we had to find distribution ourselves, which was a huge challenge, but nonetheless I love that film. It was one of those experiences in which you question why you became a filmmaker in the first place. You think *does it really have to be this hard and this painful?* The people who saw the film loved it, which was one redeeming factor, but not enough people saw the film.

DARK GIRLS

The *Dark Girls* and *Light Girls* documentaries are two of my favorite films because they deal with the unfortunate reality of conflicts within the black community. We still have the slave mentality within our own community regarding the color of our skin. It's almost like a rivalry between team light skin and team dark skin with social media hashtags and so on. In my research I discovered that skin bleach at that time was a $50 billion business. I learned that pregnant African women realize that bleaching their body can harm the baby, but sometimes they do it anyway.

I felt the film had significance because this mentality is so deeply rooted. I saw the footage of a young girl concluding that pretty and smart people are lighter skinned. This chocolate-skinned girl was placed in front of drawings of girls that ranged from very, very light skinned to very, very dark skinned and was asked to point to the pretty girl, the ugly girl, the smart girl, and the dumb girl. She pointed to the light girls as pretty and smart, while pointing at the dark girl as ugly and dumb. In her mind, everything that was pretty did not look like her. It was heartbreaking. How do we reverse this or even begin to address it? In doing research for these films, we found that it is a global issue. It's not just in the black community, but also in the Asian community. Both in the United States and in Asian countries, they hold umbrellas to shade themselves from the sun to avoid getting darker because light skin is considered more attractive. Skin bleach is a popular product in India because if your skin is darker, you are considered field-workers and lower class. If your skin is lighter, you are considered higher class. In Africa, lighter skin is considered more beautiful as well.

When I was in Ghana, I was sitting at a table with a group of people. One of the women was very light with straight hair. Something was strange about her. She always kept her hands under the table, and when she ate her food, she'd take a bite and quickly put her hands back under the table. The next time she lifted her hands, I noticed that her hand was very light except her knuckles. I later found out that the knuckles tend to be the areas that don't take to the bleach as well. This woman had bleached her entire body to look like what she thought was "beautiful."

There are two sins that the media commits: the sin of omission and the sin of commission. With commission, movies and television portray people who look a certain way playing the same roles, which sort of brainwashes audiences into thinking that's where that type of person belongs. The sin of omission is the absence of certain groups of people whenever anything of value or importance is present. For example, black people are often seen as athletes and musicians, but not often inventors, scientists, or mathematicians. We have made contributions in the sciences, but that's not seen often in the media.

I wanted to make both documentaries because it's not just dark-skinned women who face challenges. Being on the other end of the spectrum has its challenges as well. Darker women struggle with being teased and not feeling attractive. Oftentimes light-skinned women are treated like trophies and not as humans. As a result, many light-skinned women expressed not being valued for who they are but for what they represent. I wanted to make sure to explore both struggles to bridge the gap between the two and rise above this superficiality. Women are bickering over their skin tone. What really got me was the fact that skin bleaching is a $50 billion business. So many people want to change their appearance to be better accepted and better valued. That was extremely disturbing to learn. One young lady talked about riding in the car with her mother and her friend. Her mother said to the friend that she was so attractive with beautiful lips and eyes, but continued, "can you imagine how much more beautiful she would be if she were lighter?" Her mother said that without any intent of hurting her daughter's feelings. That was simply what she believed, and she had no idea what impact it had on her. That was just as dangerous.

Because of the importance of the documentary, which was nominated for an NAACP award, I created a book called *Dark Girls* that celebrated featured celebrities and other women from all walks of life sharing their intimate insights into what their dark skin meant to them. Recently, a young twelve-year-old black girl who read the book had a friend of hers call me to see if she could interview me. She and her mother came to my home. The little girl hugged me and told me that *Dark Girls* had changed her life. I cannot express how much that meant to me. Now this little girl has self-value and confidence in herself after reading the book and seeing striking photos of dark women.

If I do nothing more in this life, I know that I have changed at least one girl's journey in a positive way. Knowing that the bullies of the world can never change how this girl feels about herself gives me hope for a better future.

FALLS THE SHADOW

There has to be something wrong with a man
Who can't quite seem to understand
Why
If your skin ain't white
And your eyes ain't pearly blue
You must always carry the number two
And stand behind the bolted door and
Knock, knock, knock—then knock some more
Till your hand bleeds tracks along the floor
Of the fanged and panting corridor
That laughs you back to the crowded zoo
From whence you came
And going back, you forgot your name
And lose your way
And you meet all the strangers
And all they can say
Is
They think it's a lovely day
And slowly everything gets numb
And you don't know where it's coming from
And you get scared
To think you had a right
To rail against the black eagle night

That pushed you down its cut-glass throat
And dropped you in the gut-warm moat
Of the black child's tears
And his flat breasted mama's fears
And you can't swim and barely float to shore
When suddenly you're flushed out on the floor
Of all your dreams
That turn out to be purple jelly beans
That stick together in a clump
And you find yourself in the city dump
And hear the sizzling of straightening comb
And somebody holler: hey, you home?
There has to be something wrong.

Part V

——————•——————

NO CONCLUSIONS

My family in the 1970s (from left): My father William, my brother-in-law
John Hampton, my sister Yvonne, me, my mother Ethel, and my niece
Nalo Hampton. *From the author's collection*

Chapter 15

THE RAINBOW BRIDGE

There is no school equal to a decent home and no teacher equal to a virtuous parent.—Mahatma Gandhi

DADDY DIED, MOMMY DIED

WHEN MY FATHER DIED, I WAS making a movie called *Action Jackson* with my good friend Carl Weathers and some other great people that I respected. I had to stay focused on my work, but I also had to grieve for my father. I wasn't surprised by his passing, but I hurt deeply because I knew he was gone forever. Not only would he be buried in a grave that was deep, dark, and far away, but he would be gone from my heart, my hugs. I would never again see the expressions on his face or watch him smoke his pipe by the TV as he asked us to change the channel for him. We were his remote control in those days. He would even send us to the backyard for switches after he had spoken to us softly and tenderly about why we were getting whippings.

I felt sorrow because we had lost the king of our family; the standard-bearer of excellence. He represented manhood for me. I never thought he could die because to me he was invincible. He was muscular, strong, more than six feet tall, and never took crap from anybody. You could depend on him and he'd never let you down. He worked hard his entire life. I'm not talking about working 9:00 to 5:00; I'm talking 9:00 to 5:00 and then coming home to work from 5:00 to sometimes 9:00 at night doing odd jobs and the things that nobody else wanted to do. He did it and got paid for it. He did it not with sorrow or regret, but with pride because he was making money for his family.

I felt sadness because I was brought up during a time when I was not allowed to express my emotions. If you did express your emotions as a young man, you were called a sissy, which implied weakness. I was brought up with that thinking and that consciousness. My relationship with my father was in the context of this consciousness. We knew we loved each other but never really expressed it. I used to tell my dad I loved him, but he could not reciprocate because of the way he was raised. Yes, my father had his faults, but I miss him in many ways because he was my guide for how to be successful and how to take care of my family. I'm not just talking about my father's financial help; he took care of us and many others out of the strength of love and care that I have not seen since. He took families in and made sure they had a place to sleep, food to eat, and a doctor to see. My father helped families in the most desperate hours and wanted them to understand that they were not alone. My uncles and my father were great men. My father never served in the military and I never went, but my father served this nation. He asked for nothing and took care of his family and others. He made me a perfectionist striving for the best. My father was a quiet hero who made me the man I am today.

I had been to the hospital in Poughkeepsie to visit Dad along with my mother and sister. The doctor said my father had colon cancer deeply and thoroughly through his stomach area and we had two options: we could keep him on life support, or when his natural body functions deteriorated, we could let him go. So, my mother, sister, and I sat in this small, white-walled room together and talked about what we wanted. My sister asked, "What do you think Dad would want?" Pleading to my dad from our eyes, lips, and tongues, we decided that Dad's wishes were more important. It was decided that when it was time, we would let him go.

Before I returned to finish my film, I went to my father's room and sat there alone on his hospital bed while he was in a coma. I held his hand and cried. I didn't say much. I just looked at the bags of fluids surrounding him and draining from what once was his body. The green liquids connected tubes to his arms and legs. As I watched him drift into a deep kind of sleep, I wanted him to know that I loved him, and so I spoke awkward father-to-son words. Words of feelings, regrets, prayers, hopes, and all the things you say that have little meaning under these circumstances. They were words I hoped would help on some level, but he didn't respond. When I finished speaking, I kissed his forehead and began to leave. As I was letting go of him, he grabbed my hand and clenched it. He did not open his eyes. There were no words spoken. It was the last time I saw him alive.

At the funeral, people rose and spoke. He was loved by the community. He was our hero and he stood up for his rights as a black man in the cruel decades from the 1930s to the 1960s in cold-edged, racist Poughkeepsie. We said very little on the walk back from the burial site. I sat in the limo and cried with my mother and sister. I looked out the window and saw children playing and men and women laughing. I could see life moving on with cars, bikes, motorcycles, and pedestrians. I even saw skips in the lawns. I wanted to throw a hand grenade at it all because my soul was crying out. Didn't they know what had just happened? How could they dance, sing, and play as though nothing had changed? William Henry Hudson Duke was gone, and he took a part of me with him.

Years later, when my mother passed, I got the call from my sister while I was living in the Pacific Palisades. I fell back on the bed. I didn't pass out or faint; it was like I had been hit hard in the solar plexus. I lay there with the phone by my head and listened to my sister. I had talked to my mother just a few days prior. We had not expected this to happen. She was in decent health and I was in shock. My sister informed me that when she and my niece Nalo had visited Mama just a few days prior, she told them to come upstairs. My mother was laughing in her bed with other family members, those who had already passed away. She said she could see them around her. Among them were Uncle Albert, Uncle Jimmy, Uncle Roger, Uncle Howard, and Aunt Kate. My mother was having conversations with them. My sister and my niece asked if she was all right. My mother replied, "Go downstairs and get Uncle Howard a piece of fruit." My niece hesitated, but after my mother repeated the request, Nalo went downstairs and returned with some fruit.

My sister then convinced Mama to go to the hospital. The doctors checked her out and found nothing physically wrong, and on the way back home, my mother was telling jokes and laughing in the car. Yvonne drove up the driveway, so she could get into her wheelchair. They got inside and sat Mama in her favorite living room chair. Nalo went upstairs, and Yvonne headed to the kitchen. When Yvonne came back out, my mother was looking straight ahead with a smile on her face. She looked up. Then she looked straight until her head sunk into her chest. Yvonne said she was gone.

At first, we were angry at the hospital because they should've seen something, especially after we found out it was a heart attack. When they examined her heart, she was fine. We were angry and confused until we considered that maybe she wasn't delusional the morning of her death. Maybe she really saw all of these relatives, and they were calling her home because she was tired and ready to go. This changed my way of thinking about death. I thought that death was an ending of everything and that after you were buried, you rotted. I never thought of death as something that was a process in which you are in communication with those who have gone before you because you are vulnerable. As a result of this vulnerability, a presence comes to you and welcomes you home. I believe that death is an earthly process that we are all a part of, but there's more that's beyond our intellect, which confuses us, putting our belief systems and instincts to the test.

I think my mother was talking to someone who was there. I strongly believe that loved ones are always there, surrounding and protecting us. If we are open to this communication, they comfort us and eventually welcome us home. I think there is something much larger than our understanding. I think we are a part of something that has been here before us and will always remain.

THE PICTURE

When George Washington was born
They had a party
Chopped down a cherry tree
Did all other kinds of good stuff
But when I came along
My own mother didn't know I was here
She was asleep
So I had to come in by myself
Sure, nobody promised me a rose garden
But I just wanted at least a seed to grow
Someplace that said

"Hey, here I am, and I was planted by what's his name."
When my father died
He looked in my face like a sparrow
And it moved me so much
But
Well, my boys were there
And I was too proud to cry
So
I kept his picture upon which he had written
A few words just before he passed
And had tucked it in the inside of my shirt
And when he closed his eyes
And my mother came into the room crying
And my sister threw up
I left the room
Went to the bathroom
And closed the door
And took the picture out and looked on the back
And it said, "Boy, I love you.
I loved your momma and your sister
And I never loved anything else in my whole life
We had hard times, but I love you."
Well,
I cried in the bathroom.
I turned on the faucets so my uncles wouldn't hear me
But I think they knew because
When I came out
Uncle Albert put his arms around me
And he held me so tight
That I thought
I would never let him go

Chapter 16

———————

NOW WHAT?

Who is Bill Duke? Get me Bill Duke. Get me a younger Bill Duke.
Who is Bill Duke?—Bill Duke

FEAR AND COWARDLY EXCUSES

ONE OF THE MANY REASONS I never got married was that I always thought I was ugly, and I didn't want to have children that looked like me. I thought the reason I went through so much hell in my life was because I was unattractive, dark skinned, and didn't have the right lips or face. As a result, I didn't want children who would have to go through what I went through. I didn't want my children to come out dark like me. If I did get married, I wanted it to be someone who was white or at least someone who looked white because I thought they had it easier. I tried that for a while, and those women turned out not to like me too much. I think it has a lot to do with the psychology of my way of thinking about women, marriage, and relationships. I believe the very specific horror from my childhood that occurred is why I am the way I am today.

After my first love betrayed me, I used that as an excuse to become a scoundrel when it came to women. Somehow my inability to forgive that one person turned into distrust of any women who loved me. I think it was out of fear and self-protection. No one should ever have to pay for what someone else did to you, and to use that as an excuse for mistreating good women who loved me was cowardly. I have always been afraid of lending my heart again because I didn't want it broken and I didn't want to feel that pain again. I wanted to be in control and in charge. Many people ask me today why I'm so passionate about women's rights. Number one: I love women. Number two: I'm trying to let God know that I want forgiveness for what I have done to women in my personal life. Much of my work is to give back what I have taken. This motivated me to direct one of my latest films, *Created Equal*. This film is about a nun who wants to become a Catholic priest. I believe that women should be treated equally.

I still get those awkward questions about why I've never gotten married and never had children; it's always strange and intrusive. Some people wonder if I'm gay or if I'm a misogynist. Relationships have been a very rough ride for me. That's the truth. What I have discovered through meditation and talks with my sister and other women close to me is that I have been on a journey in terms of relationships. Until recently I never considered it a problem because I was doing what I wanted to do. I never wanted to be in a committed relationship. Of course, I am not the only man to do this. What was broken was not my relationship with women, but the relationship with Bill Duke, my love for myself, my trust of myself, and my compassion for myself. My family used to say, "don't be looking for love in the wrong places," and for most of my life, that's exactly what I was doing.

I was looking for the perfect woman who could fulfill my desires. A woman who would not make mistakes, argue or fight, or be who she was because that meant eventually she would betray me *just like the other girl did*. That is such hogwash. These women were not there when I was betrayed. They didn't do anything to me. They loved me, and I was incapable of loving them back because I do not love Bill Duke unconditionally. Why is that? Because from the time he was a little boy, he was told he was ugly, stupid, too dark, too tall, and too mean looking. I let these things roll off my back, but not off my spirit. I took some of that not to my heart but to my soul. I took some of it to the very core of my self-worth.

Not understanding that hole I was trying to fill, that hole in my soul, I dated many women to prove my manhood and my worthiness, to prove that I was attractive based upon the beautiful women with me. It wasn't until I started to heal that I began to think, *why do you need her to make you feel attractive and why don't you feel whole without her?* I tried to fill that emptiness with cars, women, money, houses, trips, clothes, and other things. My accountant said to me that most poor people spend money they don't have on things they don't need to impress people they don't know because they have little or no self-worth.

I learned that things cannot define your identity. Only you can. I don't believe anyone can unconditionally love you unless you unconditionally love yourself. They can have compassion for you and feel sorry for you, but you can't unconditionally love them unless you unconditionally love yourself. I have learned that the hard way. I've spent a lot of time alone, but I am changing that. I am changing the way I see the world based on my perception of myself and my appreciation of myself and my understanding of my self-worth. The hole that I have had in my soul all this time cannot be filled with things outside of me.

Contemplating writing this book made me do a lot of self-analysis. I went back to my childhood, but we cannot blame everything on the childhood because we are responsible for our own actions and our lives. We can't make excuses for things that happened to us as kids, but I will be honest and say there are reasons why I never had children. I never wanted to love someone who went through what I went through. I know that if I had a child, that child would look like me, dark. If it was a boy, he'd be tall and dark, and face many of the things that I've faced.

NATHALIE

I met Nathalie when she was three years old through her mother, Anna, who I was seeing at the time. Anna was from Senegal and France, and we hit it off. We had a business relationship and a love relationship. I cared for her, and I had fallen in love with that three-year-old little angel called Nathalie, who used to be the most rebellious child ever. Her favorite word was "no." Then she would smile, I would pinch her fingers, she would say "Ow" and then "OK." I loved her innocence and her beauty and her spirit and her soul. She was, and still is, an angel to me.

For multiple reasons, I never had children of my own. Work, unfortunate abortions, and other mistimings prevented that, but I always wanted a child. So Nathalie became my daughter. She's my goddaughter, technically, but she never had a father in her life until recently. I became that father figure, and it saved my life because before that I didn't really know what unconditional love was.

The first time Nathalie, her mom, and I went to a restaurant, it was an Italian place in Pacific Palisades. Her mother and I were talking about business, and suddenly Nathalie was missing from the table. I looked around and realized that she was going to other tables, putting her fingers on their plates, and even eating their food as they watched and laughed. I went over, picked her up, and told her that she had to come back to our table. When I asked why she did that, she said she liked their food better than the food we were eating.

There were challenges in our relationship during her adolescence and teenage years. Growing into adulthood and finding her way helped build the love we share to this day. She has taught me so much about forgiveness and caring and nonjudgment.

When she was little, whenever she and I were in an elevator I'd tell her not to touch the buttons. Of course, that's exactly what she would do, touch all of the buttons, and we'd stop at every floor. I'd pinch her fingers.

"Ow, you pinched my finger!"

"Yes, because you pushed the buttons. I told you not to push the buttons."

However, she's been as much of a healer to me as I have been to her. I'll never forget one of our biggest moments. I think she was fourteen and I was picking her up at a playground. She was sitting on a bench with two friends. As I drove up, I watched as she stood up, got a bottle of water, and brought it back to the boy she was sitting with. I blew the horn and she said good-bye to her friends and came to the car.

I said to her, "Nathalie, why did you get that boy a bottle of water?"

"Because he was thirsty, and he wanted it."

"I appreciate what you just did, but do you know that men treat you the way you treat yourself? I would prefer that he got you a bottle of water." She looked at me with surprise, but at the same time I think she questioned her gesture. "It's not that it wasn't kind, but it should be reciprocal. You as a young lady should be sure to let men know that a gesture of kindness is not weakness. It's a gesture of caring that you need to have reciprocated."

Nathalie is now twenty-seven and working at a nonprofit that supports older people with cancer. She's passionate about helping and doing things for others. I love and celebrate her for that. She is a selfless giver. I feel like I have contributed to the way she thinks about this world. I'm proud of that based on her actions. Her spirit was, and still is, a spirit of grace and beauty. She's a giver and not a taker. She loves life and people. She's had ups and downs, but always bounces back, and I admire her for that.

When I was in the hospital, she took time off from work and cared for me like a mother, ordering the doctors around and telling them what they could and couldn't do. Everyone in the ward was aware that there was someone in charge. It was my daughter Nathalie.

She's brilliant, caring, and beautiful. For any part I had in that, I'm proud because I love her unconditionally. She taught me that unconditional love is the most fulfilling love that any human being can experience, not only for the person they love but for themselves as well. I love her and always will, especially because things were much different during my childhood.

If you had grown up in the household that I did and saw and experienced the physical violence and verbal assaults of my mother and father's relationship, maybe you would understand. I am talking about smashing car windows with a baseball bat at 3:00 a.m., which brought the neighbors outside to watch. Then my sister and I were teased because our mother was on top of my father's car, smashing out the glass because he had crushed a light bulb against her skull after she confronted him about cheating. The police came. My sister and I stood at the screen door watching it unfold before our eyes.

HOLLAH DAYS

Christmas was always hell. My father always bought that cheap Christmas tree on Christmas Day. Those are the things you remember, the things that stay with you. Very little was put under the tree. It wasn't a day of celebration for us as kids. My mother cooked that day and people came over to eat, but it wasn't a merry Christmas for our family. In fact, we had very few merry times. My mother and father were wonderful together and loving until we were eight or nine. Something happened in their relationship around that time. I'm not exactly sure but after that, it was hell. When I say hell, I mean my sister and I didn't want to come home from school. Going to church was great because we didn't have to be at home with our parents.

That was one reason I never got married. I saw that even the marriages that worked were full of drama. I think my idea of marriage was and is unrealistic because most of my uncles and relatives got divorced. Another reason is I never knew how to approach a woman. I always thought I was unattractive and too dark, but women used to approach me. I didn't know how to reciprocate, but if they were very honest about what they wanted, whether it was sex or whatever, then we would do it. I can't remember how many times I have avoided approaching women because I always thought—especially when I was younger—that women would go after the light-skinned guys. I always thought it would be a waste of my time. To this day—well into my seventies—I still do not have the know-how to engage in conversation with a woman, which is why I spend a lot of time alone, sad. A good woman deserves to be approached. It is rare that you find someone that you get along with, who loves you, and who you love back. I am looking for that at this late age. In movies I have played pimps, but that pimp thing doesn't work with smart women because they know how dumb it is, so I can't even try that. I don't know if it was just me or other people in this business, too, but many people who approach you do so based on what you can do for them. They want something from you. I wish people would be up front so we could spare ourselves all that drama.

In my sixties, I had the same trust issues that I always had with women, especially those in Hollywood, because most women didn't want me, they wanted something from me. Not all women, some loved me, but I'd been broken. They were actresses or producers. I had been with one woman for a few years and it was a struggle because she was also in the industry. Whenever I got a job, she expected that she'd have a job, too. I put her in a couple of my films and she came to the set. The relationship worked for a while, but she expected me to make her a star and I resented it. Supporting her was not a problem, but I was not responsible for her life. I was there to support her and love her, but she expected much more than that.

If a film I was working on had all male characters, I would write a part for her or change one of the male characters to a female character. She was a good actress, on stage and in film. She'd gotten some recognition, but the relationship was as much about her career as it was about our caring for each other and after a while it wore thin. I was tired of her expectations and she was tired of me not including her in everything that I did. It was exhausting. Any success that I had, she celebrated it and resented it at the same time because she was not always a part of the movie.

So, it ended, and I really resented her. It wasn't all her fault, of course, because I knew going into it who she was. She was astonishingly beautiful, and I fell for her. The sex was great and sometimes the banter was great, but what I realized once we broke up was that we were never friends. We fulfilled each other's needs on a certain level but there was never a friendship outside of the physical attraction. There was never the unconditional love of friendship, and I had done a lot for her. Since she was beautiful, I think she felt that as long as the sex was good, that was enough. It was like she felt I should be thankful to her and that she was doing me a favor because a lot of other men wanted her.

It was hurtful when we broke up. I had gotten a play to direct and there was no part for her since I hadn't written the play. It was a great and powerful play with a great message, but she was not happy for me. She went off, saying that I didn't care about her, that I hated her, that I was jealous of her. I felt guilty because I knew what she expected, and I used that to keep the hook in her: one day maybe something I did would land her a big role. I never said or promised that, but I knew that was her expectation. I told her I'd look out for her, but that was vague, so when I got this job, it was the end of the relationship because she felt I wasn't looking out for her any longer. She left after a long speech. I was upset and angry because I felt used and abused. I was depressed for a few weeks and drank a lot of wine.

TOILET PAPER

A friend of mine pointed out that I didn't look so good, and as a result, I went to a therapist. Just fifteen minutes into my session, I vomited. It was an emotionally charged vomit due to this unhealthy relationship. All she cared about was what I could get for her or give to her. She never loved me. The therapist just sat there and finally asked if I was finished, and I said yes. He looked at me and said, "you should invest in a roll of toilet paper." I looked confused, so he repeated himself. He said, "You're really good at pointing out how bad she stinks and how bad a human being she is, but if you took a piece of toilet paper, reached back to wipe your emotional butt, and sniffed it, Bill, you would never talk about anybody else again. What you would find is that nobody stinks worse than you." I looked him in the face and said, "Am I paying you for this?" I got up and stormed out of his office.

I never saw that man again, but the most hurtful part was not that I couldn't cancel the check I wrote to him, but that after a week of contemplation, I realized he was right. He was actually right. That moment of realization was worse than when the therapist said what he said. As I've examined myself, nobody stinks more than me, emotionally, due to the issues that I bring to every relationship.

However, there's no denying that loneliness is a double-edged sword. There is the loneliness of failure and the loneliness of success. Many years ago, someone I knew had gotten divorced after fifteen years of marriage. I asked him, since he'd been married all this time, why he couldn't just work it out. He told me that he could be alone by himself. He said, "the worst thing is to feel alone with someone who is with you every day. You love each other but something separates the two of you that cannot be intellectually modified to the degree that it brings you back together." The loneliness of failure is easily understood because nobody likes to be with a loser. You have a couple of friends who are with you throughout your life. Some stay and some go, but when you're not successful, not making money, and your career is not going well in our industry, there aren't many people who flock to you.

That shouldn't be a shock, because they are hustling and trying to do what they have to do. If you can't do anything for them, you are of no use to them. It's a constant hustle because it is a pimp and ho game. If you're a ho at the time, then you're among a cluster of hos in a stable of agencies scraping and hoping and praying and pleading and sacrificing and compromising in any way that you can to get recognition that you exist and that your talent has relevance. Sometimes knocking on doors makes your knuckles raw to the bone, and the bone breaks and it cripples your self-worth.

There are many ways people try to dig their way out of that feeling. For me it was debauchery. You're just hoping that one day you'll be successful and then with the grace of God, luck, hard work, and relationships, success comes. You start making money and you go to events like the Oscars and the Emmys and the Grammys. You keep making money and meeting people in high places and driving nice cars and living in big houses. With success comes other challenges like loneliness. There are few who stay in your life whether you are up or down; I have not found this to be the majority of people I have known. My family used to call them the woodwork people. When you are doing well, they come out of the woodwork to celebrate and share in your accomplishments, but when you are not doing well, they go back into the woodwork and you don't see them until you're doing well again.

Success is not all that it seems to be. So many people love you and want autographs. There are a lot of wonderful things about that. You receive all the recognition that you ever wanted, but with it comes times of anguish. Amidst the recognition, you can still be lonely. I'm not just saying being alone in isolation, but being alone with people, men or women, who say they love you. A lot of their attention toward you is based on their needs and requests. Trying to distinguish this makes you so tired that it puts you in a climate of isolation. You literally want to be alone in a place where you can sit down and learn how to love yourself not out of ego but out of self-regard.

I've learned that it's important to be able to love yourself unconditionally. Deep in my heart, I love and respect myself, even though I have to learn more about how to love the person I see in the mirror. I think it is a lifelong goal as you age. You're not the young person that you used to be. Young, successful people are alone also. I have found that my appreciation of myself is essential because whether anyone else loves me or not, I love myself. Everybody else is a secondary consideration. There are certain holes and voids that other people cannot fulfill for you. You have to find a way through God, meditation, or another healthy way of appreciating yourself. Yes, it is a period of isolation, but it is more importantly a period of self-appreciation, self-regard, and self-respect.

DUKE MEDIA FOUNDATION

Maybe that's one of the reasons I started the Duke Media Foundation. So I could make a difference and leave something behind. I have always understood the plight of low-income children of this world, and particularly in this country. In the past, I would send donations to various organizations whenever I could. I wasn't seeing the progress that I wanted to see, which was quite frustrating, so I stopped donating. Then I realized that it was easy to complain and judge what other people were or were not doing. The difficult question was, what am I doing to make a difference? Am I just going to complain and observe and critique, or am I going to make a difference? The only way to truly make a difference was committing to action. So I decided to start my own foundation. I spoke with my friend Carl Gilliard, who has been helpful from the very beginning and continues to be. Several of my friends encouraged me, but I had to decide exactly what I wanted to do that could really make a difference.

First, I focused on attracting students who had serious interest in technology and show business. I also wanted to make sure they were interested in going to college. I wanted to help prepare them for educational success. We started with high school kids between the ages of fourteen and eighteen. First, we wanted to be able to offer them helpful information. Second, in order to enter the program, their parents had to be committed to the process as well. Parents had to pick the kids up, drop the kids off, and sometimes attend classes. The parents also had to be present and participate in the interview process. Without parental involvement, progress and help can go only so far. Based on my experience, I wanted to narrow the program down to two basic categories: media literacy and financial literacy.

A lot of young people who come to Hollywood still think we are in the film industry. We are in the media industry, from cell phone apps to video games to online distribution, webisodes, and podcasts. When I was coming up, the Internet did not exist, but now it does and it has changed the name of the game. Young people can discover themselves by gathering eyeballs and viewership for their own content. With viewership and a loyal audience comes advertising and network attention.

I want to make sure students understand the industry, how it has changed, and what it has become. They know their cell phone apps, but do they know about that new sector of jobs that exist in technology such as coding, programming, and designing? For the most part, those jobs are not held by minorities, and hopefully the foundation can help to change that. Even if students want to go into acting, they have to understand the business of acting in addition to the craft of acting, such as training and auditioning. They have to understand the discipline of acting. The Duke Media Foundation brings in professionals to teach many disciplines related to the industry. We also inform them about which colleges specialize in their interests, since not everyone is drawn to entertainment.

The second focus of the foundation is financial literacy. I was never taught how to use money. I was just taught how to spend it. As a result, I made many stupid mistakes. When I got money, I spent it. I didn't save it or invest it for my benefit. I was so used to being poor that when I had money, I spent it on things I'd never had, but I was never taught how to leverage money for the future. So I wanted to make sure that financial literacy was one of the focal points of my foundation. I want these children to understand the use of money. For example, what is the FDIC, Federal Reserve, the stock market, Wall Street, debt, credit, compound interest, and savings?

That's how I hope to make a difference. Education. I was inspired by something Kevin Durant said when he won the NBA's Most Valuable Player Award. He stood on the stage, very emotional, and expressed how much he appreciated the award but made sure to clarify that the real MVP was his mother because there were many nights when he and his brother went to sleep with their stomachs full when hers was empty. She sacrificed herself for them. Then he went over to his mother and gave her the trophy.

Our organization has been successful to an extent. I funded it out of my own pocket for several years but was able to stop doing that when we began to receive funding. My goal is to create a strategic alliance with corporations or funders to make it a national organization. I know it's a big dream, but I still want to try to make it happen. We have an obligation to give children the best that we can, because they truly are our future. The Duke Media Foundation is important to my very soul. It is my real legacy.

MEN LIKE ME (PART 4)

Men like me
Saw mama's head sliced open with a light bulb
Clutched in daddy's blood-stained hand called
Marriage
We felt mama's razor words cut the heart
From daddy's chest and somewhere deep
Inside we hide the rest
Of the sweet sweet
Childhood memories of
Those ever present
Summertimes that
Somehow hold the keys
To all we cannot rhyme
Men like me

A LIFE OF LESSONS

The wise man does not grow old but ripens.—Victor Hugo

SO MANY PEOPLE MOTIVATED AND INSPIRED me throughout my life, often in ways I never imagined possible. Educators like Dr. Hall and Lloyd Richards helped me to learn about motivation and human compassion. When people showed me kindness and concern without expecting anything in return, it showed me that I had a lot to learn about life beyond my somewhat isolated existence in Poughkeepsie, New York.

My idols like Miles Davis, Dick Gregory, and many others believed that something larger than their own lives had chosen them to help free their people from a life of suppression. They were willing to die for the cause, and many of them did. These people, along with many others, stood up and *told the truth*. Because our people have been lied to by so many, telling the truth made them leaders. Their truths also gave hope that something better could happen. I feel as though they have asked us for something. They have asked us to love ourselves as much as they did, make the sacrifices necessary for survival and self-regard.

The legacy we leave our children is based upon what we do today, not just what we do tomorrow. We cannot punish ourselves for what we have done or have not done because our humanity is always full of defeats and successes. We must continue to understand that we have an obligation, a responsibility, a duty to the next generation of children, no matter what color they may be. We have the duty to give them something that enables them to make a better life for themselves than we had. We are surrounded by a world of suffering with wars, famine, and poverty.

WRITING

What helped me learn how to keep life in perspective, at least in a way that I could creatively process it, was to become a writer. As a writer of plays and poems, I went through a process of growth. When I first started writing, I wrote down ideas and frustrations. I wrote my concepts of things and how that made me feel. I knew it wasn't polished, but I've learned that many writers go through this process to a certain extent because it is safe. You are describing your idea of what you should say, your intent, your vision, and your ideas. There is nothing wrong with that because no matter what the idea is, you have to apply structure: a beginning, middle, and end. The order can be middle, beginning, end or beginning, end, middle. That's up to you. Just remember that you have to be able to apply structure so that other people can understand it.

You have to take into consideration that someone may read your writing, if that is your goal. In preparation to write, the best way to learn is to read as many diverse authors as possible. I read about a lot of writers like T. S. Eliot, Edward Albee, Langston Hughes, James Baldwin, and W. E. B. Du Bois. At first, I was frustrated with the process. I studied the words, structure, and history of these writers. I went back and read their early works to see how they progressed into brilliance. I could never figure out why my work was so different. Was it because I wasn't as talented or skilled? Was it because I'm black and there weren't nearly as many successful black writers as there were white writers? All these thoughts went through my head.

I was brought up in an era of segregation. It was a time of great difficulty because I witnessed racism in the mistreatment of my family. I witnessed the conditions under which we were raised. I witnessed and experienced insults and beatings. I grew up hating white people because they were the enemy. There were many derogatory words we used to describe white people. I witnessed and lived through the injustices that they put black people through. I hated them for this. It wasn't an abstract hate. It was hate created by experience. I lived through the murder of Medgar Evers. I saw the deaths of so many Emmett Tills. I had an understanding of the lynchings and pure hatred. I grew up knowing who my enemy was and what I had to do to survive. I knew that I always had to be better and work harder. My parents reminded me that "nobody is ever better than you, but remember you are never better than anybody else."

That is one of the reasons I love my mother and father. They were pragmatic even though they knew what I would face as a young black man growing up in America. They tried to prepare me as much as possible for what they knew I would face. My sister and I went to a predominantly white elementary school, junior high school, and high school. We were always the minority. We were always picked on. We were always made fun of. These experiences shaped me in terms of my overall understanding of life as a young black man in America living in a white system filled with bias, prejudice, and racism.

Those experienced shaped my writing as well, especially as I matured and learned more about human nature. Despite my hatred for white people, I had white friends in high school. It was a bit confusing because even though we were in an era of segregation, I was in the band with my white friends. We couldn't play instruments very well, but we had a good time together. It was confusing because they were supposed to hate me, but they didn't. We were having a good time, and they didn't make fun of me. I didn't know how not to hate, but I knew that not every white person fit my assumptions.

One day, Lloyd Richards asked me what I was writing. I told him I was writing things that I believed in. He looked over some of my stuff and said it was missing something. I was almost offended because I thought he was going to say it was horrible, but he replied, "After reading this, I know what you think, but I have no idea how you feel." Before that point, I never thought about writing in that way. I wrote ideas and concepts, but the dangerous task of vomiting out—in nonsequential, disjointed order—what I felt was terrifying. It took me a few weeks of self-reflection to fully grasp his meaning. I had heard what he said, I thought it made sense, but when I started writing again, I wasn't able to do it.

As part of my writing process, I'd plan out what I was going to write the night before. I would plot it out and try to mimic the structure and style of others like T. S. Eliot, but I had no style of my own. I started to realize that "style" is an emotional commitment to what you're doing, and I didn't have that commitment yet. As a result, one day when I had no idea what I was going to write, I just sat at my desk and put the pen on the paper. Ten minutes went by. Thirty minutes went by. Then an hour went by and still there was nothing on the paper. My frustration progressed to anger. I was convinced that my mentor was wrong. After two hours, I was sitting there wondering what was going to happen. I started to get up to leave. Then I'd sit back down. After about three and half hours later, I got up, walked out of the room, got something to drink, and came back.

When I sat down this time, I moved my pen around a little, and something magical happened. Words came not from my mind, but from my emotions and feelings. I wrote how angry I was because of the fact that I couldn't write and how disappointing it was. I felt anger toward every teacher who never taught me how to write. What I realized was that as a writer, I was very protective of my feelings. I was afraid because in writing about my feelings, I was not in control of the shape of what I was writing. It was stuff that came out of me that I had no idea was there in the first place. There were regrets, tears, and relationships I didn't want to expose to anybody because they were so personal. I didn't want people to know the mistakes I had made in my life, my frustrations with women, my feelings about my family, my hatred toward racist white people, and my disappointment in myself. These were all things that came out in my writing. They had no shape, no syllogistic order, or framework, but they were real.

Once my truth began to spew out, I had to go back and shape it. I had already studied structure, but what came out of me, I had to edit. I didn't start with the edit. I ended with the edit. And it wasn't the editing of thoughts; it was the editing of myself. For the first time, I wasn't trying to hide my feelings; I was putting forth my feelings with clarity. It was terrifying because I was exposing my personal feelings to other people whom I didn't know and who didn't know me.

I was finally doing something I was never taught to do in my life. I was being vulnerable. My writing had been selective in terms of what I said and how I said it. It was a new experience of exposing myself in a raw way. I'm not going to say it was pleasant with a heavenly flow of blossoms floating from the sky and I was redeemed and everything was wonderful. No. It was difficult. It was guessing when I would have the courage to do it again. It brought back painful memories and I didn't want to go back there. Initially, I went back to my old tendencies. Then I would reread what I wrote without editing and a revelation came to me. I felt something. I felt the feeling that I was writing, and since that time, I have tried very hard not to go back to my old protective tendencies of writing.

A format I really enjoy is writing poetry. When someone comes to me with a script, I work with them to shape it structurally. There's a great book by Stephen Pressfield called *The War of Art*, which is such a brilliant and truthfully honest piece of work. He says that the enemy of all writers is procrastination because writing is an isolated phenom. You sit alone, all by yourself, isolated from everything in the world. No television. No nothing. You sit down with a pen and paper or a recorder or a typewriter or a computer and you write whatever comes through you. The problem with writing is that it is a lonely and often frustrating business. Many writers face writer's block; because, I think, the greatest enemy of writers is the intellect. Once you've done your research, you have to digest it, and then it has to come out through your work. The ego and the intellect can block that. According to author Richard J. Hart in his book *Edging God Out*—or EGO for short—we are our own worst enemy. We edge God out, and God is that spirit within us that can do anything. Everybody who has ever acted, written, directed, produced—even anyone who ever ran a marathon—finds out that at some point in the process, something else takes over, something bigger than us. It comes from a place that is not intellectual. Something flows through you: a spirit or vibration. Whatever that force is, you have to trust it.

HARLEM KNIGHT

The old-time radiator hissed
And gurgled
Clanked and banged
Us awake
Our alarm clock
Eyes open slowly
Peeking through cat licks
That pasted them closed
Didn't want to hear nobody say
Uh-uh

Wasn't nothin' good about
Gettin' up in the cold, steamy dampness
Of Harlem

As you moved down 7th Avenue
Toward the subway
Garbage
And last night's blood and vomit
From the excitement, the excrement, the escapement
You heard from the safety
Of your sagging out
You and her were thankful
That this morning
Although not welcome,
Had come

In the cold of 125th Street
You kissed her cheek
She smiled
And moved toward her labor destination
Past eyes
That stared like zombies
From their sockets
At her dark legs
And sweet lips
Bouncing softly
And you knew
That if ever you would lose your life for someone
It would be for her

The subway screeches
Time to meet the incoming train
Heading downtown
To clothing stacked in crates
That you pull on your back all day
And

The only thing keeping you
From taking the life of the boss
And his son
With your bare hands
Is knowing
That
You'll see her again
You'll hold her again
This
Harlem
Night
In the corner of your room
So high
On the 5th floor
Of your destiny

TRUST

Trusting what is inside you is key. You may not be able to intellectually perceive or identify what it is, but you know it is there. All great artists have had this experience of an inexplicable "taking over." It is a creative process, and the only way you can stop it is if you try to shut it down. For example, if you are an actor, there are words that you memorize, but to bring the character alive you have to regurgitate it in your own way. It is something coming out of you, and that is what writing, directing, and acting is. It's that creative energy, that spirit within, and you write it on the page. Then you can edit it later. It may not come out as clear as you want it to be, because it's initially from your emotions, but when you trust something larger than your intellect, that's when the magic begins.

It's sound odd to describe, but it's one of those things you know is inside of you. It is the trust of your own soul. How many people tell you that you can't do something? Or you're not worthy enough? Or that you don't know what you're talking about? You're too *this* and you're too *that*? They are all outside influences that can discourage and derail you, but the key is trusting yourself. That doesn't mean you don't study writing or directing or producing or acting. Far from it. Of course you need to study structure and other concepts so that you can present your talent in the right format. You need both structure and understanding, and even more so, you need courage. The courage to believe in yourself and your ideas. You have to believe in your validity, your self-love, your self-worth, and your self-acceptance. Nobody else in this world is like you. There may be similarities, but nobody is just like you. You have value, and if nobody has validated that for you, it is time for you to validate yourself. Let your soul and your spirit out in your writing. Tell the truth of your experience in life through your writing. Writing forces you to love yourself and let out your truth. It takes courage, but the payoff is something that you cannot spend.

I wish I could say that writing this book was inspired by me and my courage, but the truth is that it was not. For many years, people told me that I should tell my story because of all that I had gone through in Hollywood, but I never believed that I had anything important to say. I thought a lot of people had gone through what I had gone through. I didn't think there was anything special about Bill Duke in Hollywood. However, when I reached my seventies, I wanted to leave something for those who come after me to benefit from, because people like Gordon Parks and Michael Schultz helped me. I want to do the same thing in my own way. The Sidney Poitiers, Lloyd Richards, and Alex Haleys left something. They left a trail for us to travel down because they cared enough to speak about what they had been through so that others would not be discouraged. These people inspired me not only as a writer, but as a human being.

Black people who came before me went through the pain of segregation and were forced into stereotypical roles. I remember Stepin Fetchit. He was referred to as an embarrassment to the race, but the older I got, I realized that it was the only work that he could have gotten at that time. He did well with what he had. I'm not saying that character portrayed blacks in the most respectful way, but he did the best he could with what he had to work with. When you face the challenges of this industry—even if you are successful—you are always under the microscope, under intense scrutiny from others as well as yourself. You're always being judged, not just financially, but in terms of your relevance. You're not accepted for you. It's always about what you can bring, usually in the form of revenue. When

Louis Gossett Jr. and Mo'Nique received their Academy Awards, everyone thought their careers were going to last forever. In this business, there are no guarantees.

I hope what I have shared in this book provides a better perspective on this industry. I don't know everything, but I do know what I have been through, what has been done to me, and how I have come out on the other side. If there's anything I can leave to others, it's that through everything I have done—acting, directing, writing—I've learned that trusting my instincts and having the courage to be vulnerable are when I've done my best work. I may not leave behind amazing music like some of my heroes or inspire a generation to make a cultural change like great activists have done, but through my work and my relationships, both personally and professionally, I feel that in my own way, I'm leaving something positive for others. That might be something as simple as a meme from a movie I acted in or as complex as a passion project like the documentary *Dark Girls*.

What I've realized is that it's not so much the delivery, but the message that makes a difference. Through all of my projects, I've left a part of myself for others to explore. That's all I can do. It's up to the audience to decide what they take from it. By presenting myself in so many different ways—through acting, directing, producing, and writing—I hope people get a good idea of who I am as a person, what I've been through, the things I've experienced, and how that has manifested itself in my work.

After all, maybe people of all races can learn something from the life of a man like me.

POEM TO THE WORLD

When lovers
On the brink
Of
Finding out
Recline on
Fat illusions
Of their words
And utter platitudes

Instead of shouts
Forget
Tender silences
They've shared
And all confessions
Awkwardness they've dared
Like
Children peeking softly from their doubts
There comes a time
Of
Darkness and despair
When moments seem
Like hours under weights
Regret and fear
Like
Garbage fills the air
And lips of fondest memories
Turn to hate
When lovers
On the brink
Of
Coming near
Forget
The bodies swelled
And
Aching cries
And
Substitute excuses for their tears
Something soft
And silent in them dies
And
That, perhaps, is why there are old men
On benches
All alone
In city parks
And

Boney-fingered spinsters with hard sad eyes
Knitting things for babies in the dark
And
Maybe why we're lonely
In the spring
When
All the earth her fat thighs open wide
To show us her pretty underthings
And
Laughingly invites us to her side
To
Kiss away the differences we've known
With the tenderness
And
Wisdom of her groans
Yet
We
Lie beside each other
In despair
While
Our bodies
Make love
In
The air

INDEX